The Nature, Dignity, and Mission of Woman

The Nature, Dignity, and Mission of WOMAN

Fr. Karl Stehlin

Translated by Michael J. Miller

Angelus Press

2915 Forest Avenue | Kansas City, MO 64109

Title of the German original: *Wesen, Würde und Auftrag der Frau*
© 2009 for the English edition by Fr. Karl Stehlin, FSSPX
Published by Te Deum Sp., Warsaw, Poland

Library of Congress Cataloging-in-Publication Data

Stehlin, Karl, 1962-
 [Wesen, Würde und Auftrag der Frau. English]
 The nature, dignity, and mission of woman / Fr. Karl Stehlin, SSPX ; translated by Michael J. Miller.
     pages cm
 Includes bibliographical references and index.
 ISBN 978-1-937843-22-9 (alk. paper)
 1. Women--Religious aspects--Catholic Church. 2. Catholic women--Religious life. 3. Catholic women--Conduct of life. 4. Catholic Church--Doctrines. I. Title.
 BX2347.8.W6S7413 2013
 248.8'43--dc23
                                          2013014491

ANGELUS PRESS
2915 Forest Avenue
Kansas City, Missouri 64109
Phone (816) 753-3150
Fax (816) 753-3557
Order Line 1-800-966-7337
www.angeluspress.org

ISBN: 978-1-937843-22-9
FIRST PRINTING–June 2013

Printed in the United States of America

Contents

Foreword

Man and woman, father and mother, love, marriage, family: these are concepts which, since the sexual revolution in the 1960s, have been called into question, if not diluted beyond recognition. Gender, they say, is not determined by biology but rather by society, while "male" and "female" behaviors are "roles" in which people have been trained. In order to overcome society's "unequal treatment" of men and women, all the resources of the mass media have been enlisted to tell us that all differences whatsoever between male and female must be abolished. "Gender mainstreaming" is the name of this ideology, which is promoted by the authorities of the European Union and at the national level.

Because of the large-scale diffusion of such theories in all sorts of media, one can hardly escape it: The statement that men and women not only have equal dignity but are the same is accepted today almost without question. This ultimately results in men and women who are becoming or have already become utterly unsure about their identity and specific character and thus also about their purpose in life. In such arbitrariness and indefiniteness they lack orientation; there are no standards with which to come to terms.

Every year, during a three-day spiritual retreat, the students of Sankt-Theresien-Gymnasium [St. Theresa Preparatory School for Girls] are challenged to reflect on the meaning of their lives and on questions about character formation and the development of their personal talents. The students appreciate these days of silence very much, since it is an opportunity for them to become acquainted with intensive prayer and meditation and also with themselves and all their weaknesses and strengths. These talks on the dignity and mission of woman were presented within the context of those spiritual exercises. They made a deep impression on the girls. The following comments of one student speak on behalf of the enthusiasm of them all: "We have already heard many good talks about the dignity of woman and the different callings of man and woman. Yet, with regard to the vocation to the priesthood, I have often said to myself: It's a shame that I'm not a man. But now, after these talks, I said to myself: How proud I am to be a woman!"

We are very grateful to the Reverend Father Stehlin for compiling these talks about the dignity and mission of woman in this book. They indicate a profoundly Christian orientation and standards which are valid throughout the centuries and for all eternity.

By no means do they suggest, however, that women should go back to being "confined" to the "hearth and home." Rather, they are about the goodness and beauty of the plan which God has carried out by creating human beings as man and woman. They are about love, which finds its happiness and fulfillment in the completion of one's own being through the particularity and distinctive nature of the opposing sexes. And they are also about the rules of conduct which automatically follow from the sublime dignity of this creative plan.

May this book find a wide readership, especially among young people.

Sister Maria Michaela Metz, Principal
Schönenberg, May 15, 2009
Feast of St. John Baptist de la Salle

Introduction

Framing the Question

There comes a time in the life of a young person when he begins to ask himself: "Who am I, really? What distinguishes me from other people, from the things around me?" Usually it is the stress of the first painful experiences of life that causes him to ask further about the meaning of everything: "Why am I the way that I am? Why am I in this situation? Why am I living in precisely this time and at this place?" And at some time or other the moment comes when one gains an awareness of one's sex, often by confronting the opposite sex and experiencing the difference, indeed, the opposition between the two. Not uncommonly a girl arrives at this question because she feels at a disadvantage compared with the boy and perhaps jealously notices that he is stronger. She notices that out there in public life a man is much less exposed to danger and is much more entitled than a woman. After all, even today he plays the leading role in cultural and political life, and the whole Church is governed by men only. No wonder a girl then experiences the desire to be like a man herself; indeed, she no longer enjoys being a woman at all.

This little book is an attempt to answer these questions which every girl asks herself in the quiet hours of her life. Unfortunately a human being today is often no longer capable of taking the time to grasp things in the depths of their nature. People want immediate solutions for the here and now, which are then offered by the superficial mass media that flatters their pride. Human nature, however, is much deeper than this momentary transient living. The mystery of woman is an eternal value, and one can grasp it only by exploring the depths of its nature.

The Language of Symbols

Now we can look at a human being, man or woman, from different points of view. Woman and her problems are often the subjects of discussion. Scholars identify psychological matters or deal with the historical development of woman's status in society. They investigate the biological differences between man and woman or scrutinize relations between them from the sociological perspective. All these observations, however correct and important they may be, cannot yield the profound answer to the question of woman and her problems. They see characteristics of woman but not her nature. They see behaviors but do not explain why or for what purpose they belong to women. They observe the rays but not the source of light, the sun from which all light proceeds.

True and ultimately meaningful information about the nature of things can only be given by the One who designed them and called them out of nothingness into being. Only when we see the mystery of woman as God sees her have we discerned the whole truth. And only on the foundation of truth can we construct a true life. If we do not have this foundation, then we are at the mercy of the appearances, the illusion, the deceit and manipulation of demonic powers that are opposed to the order established by God.

If we want to look at things in the light of eternity, however, we run into a problem: how can we perceive eternally true values and timeless realities with our limited intellect? How can we express what is timeless in our language, which is bound up with the dimensions of space and time? For example, how can a human being who loves another express this love to the other? Love, after all, is something timeless and boundless. Everybody knows the answer: we make use of various signs, images, gestures, symbols, and analogies. Thus one gives the beloved a beautiful flower; one extends one's hand; one kisses him. Through these visible gestures one expresses an invisible reality. If we could not see the symbolic character of such gestures, then they would lose their meaning and would even become nonsensical.

Then shaking hands or pressing one's lips to those of another would be little more than an occasion for spreading pathogens.

Moreover there are things or objects in human existence that have a twofold meaning, in the foreground one that is material, immediately evident, empirical, and useful for everyday life: for example clothing, headgear, candlelight, food, and all the things that are necessary to maintain life. At the same time, however, they have a more profound meaning, a spiritual, invisible, and thus symbolic meaning that defines their deeper nature and expresses the inner life: a candle is not only necessary as a source of light and warmth; it also symbolizes sublime spiritual realities. So does a festive meal insofar as it is an event in community life and a symbol of the ties among members of a family. For a woman, her hair, a veil, and various ways of dressing have a deep, symbolic meaning. Therefore if a human being, especially a woman, becomes aware of the deeper meaning of these things, she will see the world and her own life with completely different eyes. When she eats she will try not just to nourish herself, but also to live in community with her family and friends. When she dresses she will not just protect herself from the cold, but will also express somehow through her clothing her inner riches. The symbolic view of things thus leads her into the depths and allows her to perceive her nature, her dignity, and her mission. Moreover, since all these symbolic things are externally visible, she places these values which are hidden in them not only before her own eyes, but also before those of her fellow human beings, not infrequently performing in this way a great service for them.

But what is true of the symbolic power of various signs, gestures, and things is true for a human being as such. In his visible existence man ceaselessly expresses invisible realities; he himself, as the "image and likeness of God," is the symbol of invisible divine realities. In particular, masculinity and femininity are profoundly symbolic: they are an expression of eternal, divine realities. To the extent that one understands the symbolic meaning of creatures, one perceives them in their whole depth, in their innermost truth. But in doing so one must never forget that this innermost depth is a realm which infinitely surpasses our ability to comprehend. Even if we can recognize what is true and somehow express it, we see only its externals, which give us some inkling of the ineffable depth before which we stand speechless, like a mountain climber who was plodding the whole time through thick fog and suddenly steps into the sunlight and can look above the clouds at the magnificent peaks.

The Human Being as the Image of God

God created mankind as man and woman. Woman is first and foremost a human being. Prior to any distinction between the sexes, the essence of man and woman is "spirit in flesh"—an immortal soul in a body that is quite uniquely animated by a particular soul, a rational animal. The human being is created by God, in God, and for God as "his image and likeness" (cf. Gen. 1:27). The human intellect is a pale imitation of the all-wise intellect of God; the human will mimics God's almighty will. The human being is privileged to depict, imitate, re-present and, so to speak, copy in creation what God is in His boundless eternity. As the ray of sunlight somehow faintly depicts the power and beauty of the sun, and as the stream of water reveals the hidden power of the spring, so too the human being should reveal God. That is what St. Paul means when he says that man should be "the praise of the glory of God" (cf. Eph. 1:12), the laudatory revelation of His eternal beauty.

Yet a creature in its limitations can reflect only several of the many aspects of the divine realities. That is why God created human beings in two different sexes: as man, a human being is able to image certain attributes of God, while as woman a human being can image other contrasting attributes: for example, a man images God's justice; a woman, God's mercy; and mankind as the union of man and woman, God's love.

The fact that man is an image of God is evident chiefly in three respects: in reference to man's origin, in reference to his goal, and in reference to the way that leads to the goal. As far as the origin is concerned, the creation account already gives us a profound insight as to how God created man in His image in one way and how in turn He created woman in another. With reference to the goal, eternal happiness, the teachings of the mystics in particular show us how differently man and woman regard eternal union with God. The way to the goal, the specific mission of man on earth, consists generally in his receiving at every moment from God "life, movement, and being" (cf. Acts 17:28), and furthermore the light of truth, divine graces, and God's instructions and commandments. If he freely accepts and assimilates these means of salvation and strives to do God's will, then every day is a stage along the journey home to God, to the eternal goal. Now this return to God, the fulfillment of our mission on earth, again differs for a man and for a woman.

Before we look more closely at the nature of woman on the basis of these fundamental observations, we must state as a matter of principle that in both cases the origin, the goal, and the way are the same. However different the missions of the two may be in their particulars, in general and essentially they have the same nature: man and woman stand as human beings before God, endowed with the same gifts, destined for the same goal. And the fact that a human being belongs to one sex or the other does not determine which of the two will one day rank higher, but rather the degree of his or her fidelity and devotion to God.

These preliminary reflections are so important in order to adjust at the outset the common, all-too-earthly comparisons between the two sexes. In God's sight man and woman are equal. The person who will be closer to God and more filled with God for all eternity is the one who has loved the most, that is, the one who has best accomplished God's will. Only during the short preparatory phase of our swiftly-passing earthly pilgrimage is there a hierarchy of sexes according to God's wise ordinance, namely subordination and authority. God wishes His glory to be represented and imaged in the world in this way.

These considerations also make it clear that the various views of woman are profoundly dependent on a correct understanding of the nature of a human being. If a worldview lacks a reference to God as the final goal, then it can only attribute a this-worldly meaning to man; that is, it cannot regard him as the image and likeness of God, but rather as a monad, the product of chance or an autonomous construct that is its own origin and end. In such a worldview it is logical that everyone strive to be stronger, more powerful, more influential, or at least just as entitled as anyone else. The ideology of women's liberation is also based on an atheistic view of the world and humanity. It leads to the effort to eliminate the differences between man and woman at every level. Aside from the fact that this leveling is contrary to their nature, the proponents of this worldview should at least take into account the physiological reality that demonstrates down to the smallest detail the immutable difference between the sexes. Indeed, a man can never bring children into the world, and it is just as impossible for a woman to assume the characteristics of a man and vice versa. When this is attempted it necessarily leads to a degenerate or monstrous result. Such ideologies are opposed by the very instinct for self-preservation and ordinary common sense. Therefore let us take as given the fundamental ways in which man and woman differ and allow God to give us the answer to the questions why and for what purpose.

Man and Woman—
Image of God

God's Unity Imaged by Created Contrasts

When we inquire about the nature, the meaning, and the purpose of a work of art, only the artist can give us the final answer. Since we are created by God and receive everything from Him and thus are completely dependent on Him, only He can give a valid answer to essential questions about our existence. "God created man in His own image and likeness; male and female He created them." Man is created to be God's own image, that is, to imitate and to represent God's nature in himself. Since we are nothing and have nothing in and of ourselves, we can attain the perfection of our being only to the extent that we are receptive to everything that God gives us. Now God wants to reveal His nature and thus to be present in His creation through His images. But how can a finite creature image, imitate, and represent the Infinite?

God is eternal unity; He possesses Himself and eternally comprehends the universe within Himself: He is the All-One. The great philosophers summarize this in two lapidary principles: *"ens a se,"* Being from itself. God is *"ipsum esse subsistens,"* Being itself, which eternally exists and sustains itself. In contrast, everything created is composed of different elements which do not exist independently but are only created by God: the creature is *"ens ab alio,"* being from something else, namely, from God. God establishes the created being by putting together the different elements and by giving it being at the moment of their union. Thus material things are composed of matter and form, which shapes the matter into a specific thing. Man is composed of body and soul, whereby the soul is the vital form of the body. Therefore if the composite creature is to be an image of God's unity, it can be so only through the manifest union of contrary elements which by complementing each other point to God's unity, which surpasses all understanding.

Take for example God's omnipresence: on the one hand God is infinitely above us; this is His transcendence, His majesty, His omnipotence and greatness, which infinitely surpasses everything created as the majesty of the mountain surpasses the grain of sand or the boundless ocean a drop of water. But at the same time God is in His creatures; He is their inmost cause, the source from which their entire being flows. St. Augustine expresses this succinctly in a Latin sentence: *"Deus intimior intimo meo."* God is more intimate than my inmost self, that is, God is more profoundly in the inmost core of my being than I am to myself. And this is His love, which desires to be united most intimately with us. Now how can human beings manifest this mystery of the one God who is in all and at the same time infinitely above all? Only through two juxtaposed, "contrary" created realities which image and imitate this unique divine attribute when they are seen in terms of or in relation with each other.

The same is true of God's inmost mystery, the fact that He is on the one hand the most definite personality—so much so that all created individuality and distinct personality is only a tiny reflection of the unparalleled uniqueness of His paternal "I" and filial "Thou." And at the same time God is a boundless ocean, an inexhaustible light, infinite universality which carries everything in itself and causes everything to rest. He is Eternal rest and inexhaustible light, as the Church's Office of the Dead puts it: *"Requiem aeternam dona eis, Domine, et lux perpetua luceat eis."* ["Eternal rest grant unto them, O Lord, and let perpetual light shine upon them."]

And again the question arises: how can man image this mystery both of the definite, unique, distinct and unmistakable Divine Persons and also of the universal, all-encompassing, endless ocean of divine Being? Likewise through the contrast of two juxtaposed creatures, one of which tends to represent the aspect of the individual, personal God who works and creates specifically, while the other represents the aspect of the universal, supportive and rest-giving bosom of divine Being. That is why God created one human nature in the contrast of the sexes, man and woman, which in their diversity represent the different attributes of divine Being and in their union again demonstrate that all these attributes in God are nothing but expressions of His indivisible unity.

God Over All and In All

Now the man is the image of God "over us," which is why he seeks the God who is "above all being" by thoroughly investigating God's work, reflecting on Him in His greatness and investigating His mysteries. He is the image of the transcendent God inasmuch as he imitates His work as Creator, His guiding and ordering of things. In the world he shares in God's authority, he is the head, the leader, the organizer. His intelligence plans things and accomplishes them. He is like the architect and master builder of a palace.

The woman, in contrast, is the image of God's loving devotion to His creation; she shows forth God as the one who is present "in us." That is why she rests in God, finds her protection, safety, and home in Him. She experiences herself as the house of God, as the chalice, the womb, the receiver, the guardian of divine life and of love. She is the one who principally rests in God, while man is the one who principally seeks God. Her resting in God enables her to be taken up into the mystery of His Fatherhood, into the primordial source of fruitfulness. Indeed, He ceaselessly works in a hidden way in the inmost depths of all being, fills everything with life, sustains, supports, and preserves His work. He blesses, cherishes, cares for, nourishes, and guards everything. According to St. Augustine, in the inmost depth of the creature He is the paternal bosom and maternal womb that bears and swells and pours forth, the primordial ground of all being. Christ goes so far as to compare himself with a servant who sacrificially gives Himself over to His creature. And God now enlists woman in particular in this loving and caring divine devotion to His creature: she can participate in the Fatherhood of God as a perpetually fruitful giver of life, as a mother. She is privileged to serve life with God and in Him, to be the source and mother of life. That is why the name of the first woman is Eve: "Mother of the Living." For this reason God gave her the peculiar features that she needs for this mission: physical strength to receive, bear, bring forth, nourish, and raise new life. He gave her the special quality of serving life and guarding and protecting it with care. Among animals there is already the start of a maternal instinct, a faint shadow of the life-giving and life-preserving power of woman. She gives to the child the gift of life and watches over its growth; she protects and sustains the man's life by being for him a hearth and home, a place of refuge and security. She is responsive to her fellow men in their need, so as to protect life that is endangered, to help the poor according to her means, and to alleviate suffering. The Fathers of the Church call her the steward of LOVE, the heart of the world.

God Who Is One and All

Man represents God in his specific personal creative activity, in the uniqueness of his individual personality. The history of mankind is profoundly marked by the influence of specific personalities, by the great individual, and as a rule this is a man. He dominates the political and cultural life of peoples and nations by accomplishing here and now his work: it is the individual deed, his specific work to which the man devotes his talent, becoming completely absorbed and exhausted by it. Thus he has a personal and specific effect on the concrete historical situation; at every turn he has the present moment in view, the specific work, the building up of the culture, the civilization, the kingdom of God.

It is quite different with the woman: exceptions aside, she appears nameless; her personality withdraws completely into the background. She represents instead the calm waters of the divine ocean, the nameless ALL of God. She presents what is general, what transcends the personal throughout history. Her essential task is not to present what is personal, like the man, but rather to receive noble values and to carry them along from generation to generation like a subterranean stream. She is the silent bearer of human values, talents, and abilities.

A man expends his strength in his own work; a woman does not expend it but rather passes it on. A man exhausts himself in his work; a woman gives away her very talent, namely to the next generation. From this perspective it then takes on a symbolic significance that the individual woman lives longer on average than the individual man: a man represents the situation at hand, while a woman represents the generation. A man signifies the value of the moment for eternity; a woman signifies the endless course of the generations. A man is the rock upon which time rests; a woman is the stream that carries it along. The rock is solid—the stream is fluid: personality belongs primarily to the man, while what is universal belongs to the woman. What is personal is unique and therefore transient—it consumes its capital, while what is universal saves it. Just as the individual woman on average lives to be older than the man, so too the female line of the generations grows older than the masculine line.[1]

Precisely this element in woman that transcends personality, this timeless power that bears life and passes it on, is the cause of her namelessness and concealment. It is significant that the great male figures of history usually owe their talent and their intellectual greatness to their mother, whose name, however, remains unknown to the world. It is precisely those mothers whose names have come down to us through the gratitude of their brilliant sons who show us their silent power which is concealed from the world: for example, St. Monica, without whom there would have been no St. Augustine; or Blessed Aleth, the mother of St. Bernard; or, in our time, the saintly mother of Archbishop Lefebvre.

Now there is a very eloquent symbol of this nameless and concealed power of the feminine nature, the VEIL, which conceals precisely what is personal about the woman (her face and hair) and emphasizes those aspects of her mission that are general and transcend the personal: every great feminine event is concealed and silent, as we will see in detail, and concealed likewise is her vital act: her gift of self to the beloved THOU, her life-giving, life-preserving and life-sustaining power as mother. Everything that is precious and holy needs a

---

[1] Gertrud von Le Fort, *Die ewige Frau* [The Eternal Woman] (Munich, 1962), 37-38.

veil, as the Old Testament already shows: The Ark of the Covenant is kept concealed behind a curtain or veil (Ex. 26:33), and while it is being transported it is wrapped in the veil (Num. 4:5). Those who look at the Ark are punished.

In church the Most Blessed Sacrament is veiled, something that is made particularly evident in the Eastern rites by the iconostasis or icon screen. The Roman rite veils and conceals the tabernacle, the ciborium, and, during Mass, the chalice.

Analogously, the veil is the symbol of woman's service to the most precious thing that there is: life. For her it is a reminder that she is most profoundly herself when she is not there for her own sake but rather is turned toward the living Thou, as bride and mother.

Another expression of this concealed and sustaining power is the woman's feeling of shame, which causes her to conceal and preserve the mystery of her beauty.

Union of Opposites

The perfect imaging by man of God's inmost nature occurs, however, only when man and woman are united in the indissoluble bond of love. According to God's will, that is their destiny on earth: "For this reason a man shall leave his father and mother and be joined to his wife, and the two shall become one flesh" (Mt. 19:5, Gen. 2:24).

This completion of both, which is willed by God, is depicted quite clearly in the creation account: at the creation of mankind the man was alone at first. He was the ruler over all creatures, the king of paradise. We see his astonishment as he discovers God's work, comes to know the nature of all things and "gives them names," which means to define their provenance, their meaning, and purpose.

Yet it was not good that man should be alone. For the most profound thing in a human being is the power to love, but one can love only a THOU, whereas all things on earth are only an "it," that is, means and helps, but not creatures that one can love. So God created for the man a helper fit for him, who can accept and internalize his devotion and then respond with the same devotion. Again and again in the following pages we will observe that precisely the interpenetration of these opposites—man and woman—reflects most sublimely God's nature as infinite love (see I Jn. 4:8).

If we return to the creation account, we notice yet another characteristic of the nature of woman as God designed her from eternity. It is conceivable that man could be alone, focused only on his task on earth and, of course, on God as the Author of all. Being alone is unthinkable for the woman, however, inasmuch as she does not exist only for herself but is always oriented toward a Thou for whom she can be a helper, someone whom she can love. Her essential characteristic is never being alone, but rather caring about the beloved Thou: the spouse, the child, the poor and weak. There is hardly anything more forsaken or absurd than a woman on her own in the midst of the whole world's magnificence, without a human being with whom she relates and who gives meaning to her life. That is why, unlike masculine nature, her royal character lies not in the ability to be utterly alone, but rather in helping and serving. And that is why she is much closer to her neighbors than the man, much more concerned about their difficulties and needs.

The union of the opposites, "God among us" and "God over us" on the one hand, and "God who is ONE" and "God who is ALL," on the other hand, becomes visible in the union of man and woman; this is beautifully symbolized by the tree. The woman is the hidden root, the supporting foundation, while the man is the visible tree top; the woman is the complete essence of the tree, submerged in fertile Mother Earth, whereas the man is the specific unfolding of the tree in all its visible ramifications. Therefore when man and woman unite harmoniously, their wedding represents the full image of God. So the family of mankind ought to be.

The Intrusion of Sin

Now we also know that God's original plan for His creation, as He designed and created it in the glory of Paradise, no longer exists. Through his fall from God's favor because of his proud belief that he could "be like God" by his own power, man lost friendship with God and ruined his interior beauty and harmony. This also plunged sexual self-worth into misery along with the rest [of creation], and disturbed the original loving relationship between man and woman. Are the preceding observations then only pointless nostalgia for something that will never be again? No. Although the wounds of original sin are terrible, they did not destroy human nature but only disturbed it. Man is still the master of the earth; its fruits are still destined for him. But it is no longer enough for him to reach out his hand; he must struggle to obtain them, bent under the difficult yoke of tilling soil that is full of thistles and thorns. Though still man's helper, woman no longer simply shares in his joy, but rather labors in a servitude subordinate to his.

Sick man, therefore, is not dead; he can be well again if someone comes to heal him. But he can recuperate only if he thinks back to what once was, according to God's plan, and is still supposed to be. The restoration of that order through Christ allows man not only to be the "image and likeness of God" again, completely and even more than before; it also restores in a pre-eminent way the essential meaning of man and woman.

The Essential Vocation of Woman

We can look at the nature and mission of woman from two perspectives. The one way, beginning from below, so to speak, consists of starting from the general experiences and feelings of woman, analyzing their causes, circumstances, and purposes and thus arriving at her genuine, inmost nature, and finally elaborating the conclusions that follow from it. This way is theoretical and abstract, yet has the advantage that it considers and investigates the mystery of being a woman in its full depth. The other way is practical and concrete, for it presents specific women who actualize the essence of being a woman to the utmost and who thus have attained the ideal. These are the great women of history, the holy virgins, mothers, brides of Christ, and martyrs. Over them all, however, looms that incomparable Lady who is exalted and blessed above all that is feminine, the Woman of all women, the Virgin of all virgins, the Bride of all brides. In inimitable fashion she is the symbol of the feminine: in her alone the entire mystery of woman has taken form and become a reality.

The feminine mystery comprises three great realities: each of them has its own value, yet the whole mystery of woman is fulfilled only in the intertwining of the three. While this fullness can be suggested here on earth, it can be fully realized only after the abolition of space and time, in eternity. The first phase of woman's existence is spent under the sign of virginity; this is the mystery of woman as such, her most authentic nature, her heart, her vital force, and thus woman considered in herself. The second aspect appears when woman attains the fullness of her physical and intellectual powers and can accomplish her mission. Here it is the bridal mystery in which a woman discovers herself as being ordered to a beloved Thou, to whom she wants to give herself, to whom she reveals herself, with whom she unites herself. The highest expression of woman's nature, however, is motherhood, which conceives, brings forth, and cares for new life as the fruit of love for the beloved Thou.

Now if we look at the contrasting nature of the masculine, then fatherhood corresponds to motherhood, and the bridegroom to the bride. On the other hand the first phase of virginity belongs to both as the revelation of their most authentic nature and the self-worth which God has placed in both creatures.

Virgo

Experiences

What does experience tell us? Woman has a profound sense of the beautiful, hence her special attraction to flowers and to the glories of nature. This is not just an enjoyment of the variety of forms, but also a grasp of the still hidden harmonies concealed in the beauties of nature. She likewise typically has a special sense for art, music, and culture, understood primarily in terms of their beauty and harmony. This concern of hers for the beauty of external things extends also to herself. How important attractive clothing and her physical appearance—particularly her hair—are in a woman's life! Her love of jewelry also testifies to her sense of beauty, which she wants not just to behold but also to wear. She wants to be surrounded and filled with beautiful things.

A second characteristic of woman is her sense of purity: it is unimaginable that a mentally sound woman would not care about the cleanliness of her body and clothing. And wherever she may be living or staying, all the rooms and objects are dusted and cleaned regularly.

A third special characteristic of woman is her sensitivity to what is healthful, fresh, and youthful. That is why signs of aging are a problem for many women: cosmetics exist to satisfy her inner drive to look young as long as possible. Even youthful women want to emphasize their fresh, young features as much as possible.

With respect to her neighbors, this womanly sense for what is fresh and healthy is evident in her care for those who are deprived of health. Although we say that a woman especially has a heart for the weak, the sick, and frail elderly persons, this often comes unconsciously from the desire to see people healthy and lively; the lack of those qualities is perceived as something that should not be.

A final experience that illustrates the feminine character is a special attachment to what is constant, firm, lasting, and noble. Once a woman has found a home it is unspeakably difficult for her to leave it again.

Whatever valuable and noble things she encounters in life remain fixed in a very special way in her memory as a deep experience of joy and happiness. One should understand her love of jewelry also in this sense. Jewelry is something valuable, and precious stones, gold, etc., have the qualities of permanence, immutability, and lasting beauty.

Now what do these specific experiences of being a woman have to do with virginity? First of all they answer the question of why a woman thinks so much in terms of beauty. We see this also in the fact that in her thoughts, wishes, and dreams she likes to compare herself with intact, blooming flowers, with a spring of pure, fresh water, with the deep blue sky full of stars, with the fresh snow on the mountains. She loves the atmosphere of untouched nature, of the beaming sun, of the cozy garden. She is delighted by a precious vase, a gleaming golden vessel. This sense for what is beautiful, pure, harmonious, sound, and constant points to a fundamental attitude, an essential characteristic of woman: she is VIRGO, virgin.

Before going on to a more precise analysis of virginity, we must first rule out a misinterpretation: generally a virgin is equated with an unmarried girl who is quite intent, however, on being the wife of a husband. If she does not have this good fortune, her situation is thought to be tragic. The proverbial phenomenon of the "old maid" is all too well known from literature. Not until the present dark times was "being single" regarded as something valuable—contentment with being alone, without ties to anyone or anything. In reality this modern concept is only a euphemism for egotism and selfishness, and in reality such individuals are slaves of their own vanity and sensuality. The fact that many of these people drift into alcoholism, drugs, and other addictions only goes to show how unhappy the state of the contentedly single woman is.

God created woman with the utmost love and care, placing within her a memory of paradise, of the pure and perfect creation as it proceeded from His hands and existed before the Fall. In an unwitting tribute to this sublime distinction, we find generally in pre-Christian history a great respect for the virgin: She wards off the curse and breaks the magic spell. Church history leads the way in praising the great deeds of virgins, but literature and art also deal with them splendidly. The result in any case is that virginity radiates an unconquerable strength and power which enables a human being to commit himself unreservedly to something great.

The fact that a virgin is untouched gives her nature an inner beauty which is often perceptible externally also in the bright, clear sound of her voice, in the harmonious form of her figure or her face, in her delicate hands, in her graceful conduct.

Virginity—Image of Divine Glory

Why did God will this miracle of beauty, the virginal creature? So as to represent in an extraordinary way the most profound meaning and value of human life, namely to reflect God's splendor and glory on earth, to be a flower "for the praise of His glory" (see Eph. 1:12). "Like the lonely flower in the mountains, high up at the edge of the everlasting snow, which no human eye ever beheld, like the inaccessible beauty of the poles and the deserts, which cannot be exploited immediately for the use and the purposes of man, so also the virgin proclaims that a creature has meaning only as a reflection of the eternal splendor of the Creator."[2]

For mankind in our time, which can think only in pragmatic terms and always asks what a thing is useful for and what effects it produces, the virgin appears to be useless. Since she renounces the

---

[2] Le Fort, *The Eternal Woman* [German], 43.

exercise of her sexual powers, her life is thought to be squandered, unfulfilled, or botched. The sacrifice that her unsullied state involves is regarded as absurd or even as unnatural violence. Hence too the world's negative view of religious life, especially contemplative life, as an "absurd, wasted existence."

The opposite is the case. From virginity bursts forth the most precious, most valuable, and most perfect gifts that can ever be granted to a human being. For example, man's body was drawn through sin into the most profound misery, and since then he has been enslaved by his passions. Christ came in order to redeem the body from this perdition: "We know that our old self was crucified with Him [through Baptism] so that the sinful body might be destroyed, and we might no longer be enslaved to sin" (Rom. 6:6). "Let not sin therefore reign in your mortal bodies, to make you obey their passions" (Rom. 6:12). "For just as you once yielded your members to impurity and to greater and greater iniquity, so now yield your members to righteousness for sanctification" (Rom. 6:19). This cleansing of bodily life by Baptism causes our body to emerge from the cleansing bath as a "new creation"; now it is made entirely holy and pure, an instrument of new life. And that is why the Christian should "shun immorality. Every other sin which a man commits is outside the body; but the immoral man sins against his own body" (I Cor. 6:18). The highest perfection of this beauty and sanctity of the body, however, is the completely intact virginal body.

In another passage St. Paul speaks about the advantages of virginity (I Cor. 7:25-40). One of them is "freedom from anxieties." By this he means that the married person is much more firmly attached to this world than the virginal person. Because of his family he is much more "interested" in the workings of this world. He is bound to the world like someone who has loaded his belongings onto a ship and is now dependent on its vicissitudes. "The married man is anxious about worldly affairs" (I Cor. 7:33). In contrast, the life of a virginal person is wrapped in a mysterious freedom which our Lord Himself describes: "Do not be anxious, saying, 'What shall we eat?' or 'What shall we drink?' or 'What shall we wear?'...Your heavenly Father knows that you need them all" (Mt. 6:31). This unconcern with worldly things enables the unmarried person to devote himself to higher and even sublime values and to develop his talents to the fullest.

St. Paul likewise says that the married person is divided, concerned about the things of this world, how to please his wife. By this he means that it is impossible for the married man to devote himself wholeheartedly to a greater cause simply because he must divide his time and energy. The virginal person, however, can be a "whole person." Precisely because a thousand different anxieties about this life do not occupy his soul and he is impelled by only one great and mighty passion that fills his heart to the brim, namely "seeking the kingdom of God," his life takes on the character of wholehearted, authentic, and total devotion. He is capable of determination, ardor, and perseverance. The virginal person dispenses with pettiness, nervousness, and anxious looking back and forth. Virginity is wholeness in the deepest sense of the word. Furthermore virginity contains within itself an inner dynamic, a characteristic movement toward higher things. Once a human being has discovered this wholeness and freedom from concern, he becomes increasingly receptive to lasting, eternal values. At the same time the swiftly fading joys of the world lose their attraction and the soul ascends more and more easily to the "everlasting hills." Just as the priest during Mass carefully surrounds the paten with all the fingers of both hands and thus lifts it up to God, so too these people lift up their whole being and nature to heaven, renewing this intention every day. It is somewhat like a mountain climber who suddenly sees from afar a magnificent mountain top and upon it a wonderful golden palace that he is to own one day. Thrilled by this splendid prospect, he ceaselessly climbs, possessed by the sole thought of arriving at his destination.

St. Paul describes the mystery of the Church as the Bride of Christ, whom He has sanctified, "that He might present the Church to Himself in splendor, without spot or wrinkle or any such thing, that she might be holy and without blemish" (Eph. 5:27). Through His Blood He has made her virginal, and virginal souls are born in her. Virginity embodies the most profound mystery of the mystical Bride of Christ; it is at her very center, where the altar is and the holy fire of Christ's sacrificial death burns perpetually. From this inmost precinct her vital energies stream forth into the world.

Virginity, Guardian of the Married State

Virginity is often set in opposition to married life. Therefore it is very important to point out that marriage itself acquires its profound meaning and fulfills its purpose in light of virginity. In other words, a marriage is worthy, good, and holy only when it is understood as a shadow and image of something infinitely higher and nobler. Marriage is an image and likeness; virginity is the full truth and reality. Marriage acquires its sublime value in light of the virginal espousal that is its prototype, the source of its strength, its ideal and goal.

In his Letter to the Ephesians (5:25), St. Paul shows the most profound value of marriage: "Husbands, love your wives as Christ loved the Church." Why does God will the bodily union of man and woman, when it has become so difficult after the Fall to keep this union from degenerating into "immorality"? He wills it so as to set up an image, a likeness, a palpable presentiment of His own love for the Church. A husband should cherish and care for his wife as his own flesh, "as Christ loves the Church." And the wife should be subject to her husband and obey him, as the Church lovingly obeys Christ. Thus this mystery, which is "great…in reference to Christ and the Church" (Eph. 5:32), is accomplished in the marriage and sex life of the spouses. The intimate, indescribably profound, love-filled union of the Lord with His Church acquires a faint, "fleshly" but nevertheless clear image and likeness in the marital union of husband and wife.

What is, then, the ideal image of marriage? First of all, the husband's body belongs to the wife and the wife's body to the husband. But in Christian marriage this mutual belonging is not simply determined by pleasure and the will, but is profoundly rooted in the fact that in their mutual love the spouses give expression to the love of Christ and of His Church. They do this through their decision to love one another as Christ loves His Church: faithfully, devotedly, self-sacrificially, indissolubly, and inseparably. That is why Christ made the union of man and woman for the purposes of marital and family life the source of graces by raising it to the dignity of a sacrament, a "holy sign" that is the source of ineffably sublime graces and gifts which we need so much "while we are at home in the body...away from the Lord" (II Cor. 5:6). The Sacraments are given to us for our earthly pilgrimage. Thus, for example, Christ already desires to be present among us, but hidden under the sacred forms. Just as Christ is present in different ways in the sacrament and in heavenly glory, so too there is a difference between the married state and virginity in the Church. Both, in fact, are based on one and the same fact of salvation: the marital bond between Christ and His Church. The difference is major: In marriage there is an image, a likeness, a "holy sign," whereas in virginity there is the full reality and perfect being. In marriage the husband is only an "image" of Christ and the wife the image of the Lord's Bride.

> Virginity, however, is the Bride of Christ completely, without image and reflection. In marriage Christ's wedding is already true and real—as He Himself is in the Blessed Sacrament of the altar—yet hidden and veiled under the appearances of bread and wine. In the virginal state, however, the wedding with Christ exists in the fullness of truth and reality, without veil or covering, pure and beautiful and magnificent, like Christ in the glory of the Father. That is why virginity is not a sacrament, just as Christ in the glory of the Father is no longer a sacrament.[3]

Virginity—Glimmering of Eternity

We are the children of our time, infected by a complete overemphasis on this-worldly things during our short life on earth. In truth, however, we are also "strangers and exiles on the earth" (Heb. 11:13) as we look forward to our heavenly homeland. "The fashion of this world is passing away" (I Cor. 7:31). Now marital and family life necessarily leads spouses to regard the cares of this world as the most

---

[3] J. Dillersberger, *Wer es fassen kann* (Salzburg, 1932), 134.

important thing. The more achievements civilization has to offer, the more it draws man's sights down to earth, so that he takes them more seriously than they really deserve. Therefore in order to restore the interior equilibrium, there must be on earth witnesses to eternity who voluntarily renounce the joys of this world; indeed, they pass so quickly that it is not at all worthwhile to cling to them.

Instead of those passing goods, these people choose the true Good, the eternal Bridegroom whom they await with longing; they are engrossed with the one thought: "The Bridegroom is coming" (Mt. 25:1-13). They are the five wise virgins. Christ is the sole object of their love; with every fiber of their being they wait for Him. They faithfully perform their daily duties, but through it all their eyes are watchful, their ears are listening, their bodies are tense, expecting at any moment "to go out to meet Him." A longing fills their heart, a great passion, a yearning for Christ, the Bridegroom.

The early Church was preoccupied with this thought; the catacombs were full of countless oil lamps, and the hearts of the persecuted Christians were lifted up to Him, ready at any moment to be led off to the arena. Their customary greeting was: "*Maranatha—Our Lord, come*" (I Cor. 16:22), and their prayer: "Come, Lord Jesus" (Apoc. 22:20), "Let grace come and the earth pass away."[4] No wonder the great holy virgins of the early Church matured in such an atmosphere. Thus the virginal women and men of all times witness to the Lord's mysterious words, "Behold, I am coming soon" (Apoc. 22:12). "If you will not awake, I will come like a thief, and you will not know at what hour I will come upon you" (Apoc. 3:3).

If the form of this world is passing away "soon" though, then "the virgins [can] follow the Lamb wherever He goes" (Apoc. 14:4) and sing to Him a new song. Their song is "new"; nobody can imitate these preternaturally clear, heavenly, soaring melodies! The ones who can sing them are those who "have been redeemed from mankind… for God and the Lamb" (Apoc. 14:4). They are called the "first fruits," the first spring blossoms of mankind, who stand "spotless" before the

---

[4] Didache, 10, 5, 6.

throne of God, and "in their mouth no lie was found" (Apoc. 14:5). "Virginity, what do you make out of the children of this earth? They are formed from dust—and you write the name of the Lamb on their foreheads with gleaming characters? And the name of the Father! 'Who are these…and whence have they come?' (Apoc. 7:13). Longing for them burns bright in our sinful hearts."[5]

We are coming to the final fulfillment, to the most sublime spectacle. The angel speaks: "'Come, I will show you the Bride, the wife of the Lamb.' And in the Spirit he carried me away to a great, high mountain, and showed me the holy city Jerusalem coming down out of heaven from God, having the glory of God" (Apoc. 21:9-10). This is the great fulfillment of the end times, when "the first heaven and the first earth had passed away" (Apoc. 21:1). Then mankind will realize that all of its paths through mud and sin, its obscure longing and its dull ambition, the everlasting battle, the perpetual parting and joining of the sexes, the most profound significance of all "historical" deeds and events, all literature and thought, all the art and high-altitude flights of the children of men—all, everything will acquire a final, magnificent meaning; because all these things, though often distorted and deformed beyond recognition, yet often in splendid purity and greatness, proclaimed and continue to proclaim one thing alone: the wedding of God with mankind, the descent of the highest, purest, eternal love into the lowliness of this earth. Thus virginity is for the world the perpetual writing on the wall signaling that man is ordered to an eternal goal, to an eternal life where "they neither marry nor are given in marriage, but are like angels in heaven," that is, in the immediacy of union with God. The very fact that they preserve all the energies of their body and soul for the one thing necessary makes virgins a sign and reminder to the world that man is created for God and finds his happiness and destination only in virginal eternity.

How important it is for a woman, especially for a young woman, to acknowledge this mystery of her nature and to live accordingly. Sin, too, which attacks the virginal mystery, which is to say, the beau-

---

5   Dillersberger, *Wer es fassen kann*, 153.

ty and integrity of a human being, cannot completely destroy this natural character. A woman cannot change her nature, even though today many, indeed, most, women no longer know themselves and wander about ceaselessly without direction or destination, becoming the playthings of illusions and deceptions, and so frivolously sacrifice the most beautiful pearls of their being to momentary pleasure. A girl who still has sound morals, however, prizes her integrity very highly and instinctively reacts against anything that could offend against her virginity. Every woman, even a married woman, still has a great yearning for this untouched beauty.

Virginity as Duty

Thus God has placed this exalted virginal character in the nature of woman. Now her free will must release these natural energies, reduce them from potential *(potentia)* to actual reality *(actus)*, in keeping with the wise saying, "Become what you are!" Through her own striving and efforts a woman must actualize this ideal image that is imprinted in the deepest part of her nature, and she must do this throughout her life. The goal of a human being on earth is to possess his humanity in its fullness; that is his perfection. And the way to this perfection is like climbing to the top of a mountain. Every stretch of the way, every day must be a stronger acknowledgment of the value of virginity, and that already is a great deed, especially at the present time, when precisely these values are despised by most people and dismissed as abnormal and insane. This acknowledgment is not enough, however: one must continuously and consciously seek this true beauty and at the same time resolutely turn away from anything that could sully it.

Negatively speaking, this means that one develops an ever greater aversion and loathing for anything that is impure, dirty, worthless, ugly, or destructive. The ugliest thing of all is sin, especially the kind of sin that poisons the sources of purity, soils the beautiful flower with dirty hands, or even tries to uproot it, and wants to destroy feminine beauty and harmony in its entirety. Specifically this means any sort of flirtation, which in practice is only out for sensual pleasure and does not respect the nature of the person and therefore does not value the woman as such but tries instead to derive pleasure from her external charms. It likewise means any exposure or abandonment of what is precious through immodest styles or the exhibition of the body as an object of pleasure. What reasonable woman would put a precious stone into a box together with worthless trinkets or treat it like a plaything, tossing it around carelessly? What reasonable man would put everything valuable that he owns at the side of the road in front of his house so that any passerby could take it away? Will he not instead hide, cover, and carefully guard his most precious goods so that no trespasser can see them, much less steal them?

Viewed positively, virginal integrity signifies harmony and wholeness, which can be established and maintained only through a sense of order. That is why virginity requires putting one's interior life in order, bringing it into that harmony in which everything has its place as God intended. According to the hierarchy of values we can rank things as Most Important, then Necessary, then Useful, and only then, finally, as Pleasant. According to this hierarchy we should plan our daily agenda and lead our whole life. This sense of order applies also to external life, namely the place where one stays and the things with which one deals. The experience mentioned earlier, that a woman has a special sense of order, cleanliness, and decorum is thus nothing but an outward expression of the mystery of virginity.

Then this positive element has to develop and unfold in everyday life through a love of what is integral, untouched, and pure. This sort of life is supported by a conviction about the sublime value of the precious gift that one has received. It is the preservation of the flower's beauty at all costs. A girl has self-esteem, reverence for her profound mystery, and demands that everyone else should respect it too. A woman will be appreciated and respected only if she does not abase herself by making herself the object of others' concupiscence.

Ideals

So far we have traveled the path to the nature of womanhood from below, so to speak: we examined a woman's everyday fundamental experiences of herself, evaluated their deeper significance, and arrived at the inner nature of virginity and the question of how to translate this into practical action. Now there is another path, mentioned above, namely reflection upon those women who have actualized this high ideal in their lives. Here we are confronted first by the host of great virgins, especially those who are closest to the present-day situation and the problems of women. Many of them were simple girls to begin with, without any education, without special aptitude, without extraordinary virtue. They had to struggle with everything that women today have to struggle with too. Some of them also suffered painful wounds, which at certain times even endangered their eternal salvation.

The virgins who suffered martyrdom for the purity of their faith and of their souls left such an impression on the Church in the first centuries that the liturgical calendar commemorates them just as it does the great Fathers of the Church. In every age the lives and deaths of Agnes, Cecilia, Lucy, Anastasia, Agatha, Catherine of Alexandria, etc., have fascinated people. In particular, adolescent girls found in their saintly contemporaries a shining example that often shaped their whole lives.

From my own experience I might mention that during my time as a missionary in Africa I met girls for whom the biography of St. Agnes was the great spiritual discovery of their lives. Thrilled by her ardent devotion to Christ, her steadfastness in defending her virginity, and her apostolic zeal for converting her fellow men, the simple lives of these African girls flowed, so to speak, into the mighty stream of this saintly virgin. This gave them the strength to resist the pressure of their pagan, immoral surroundings and even of their own non-believing families and to become in turn a beacon to others. Two or three girls of this caliber led hundreds of children to the faith.

The virgin martyrs of the early Church were followed by those holy virgins who preserved their vital energies for Christ, mainly in cloisters, and devoted themselves completely to Him. The countries of Europe owe their conversion to Christianity primarily to the missionaries, who like pioneers traveled through remote regions to bring the saving message of the Cross, but secondarily to the devoted women who offered themselves to the Lord as virgins for the sake of their families and neighbors and so obtained, down to the present day, untold graces for their people and therefore became the patroness of their country. Examples are St. Ottilia, St. Genevieve, St. Barbara, and St. Dorothy.

In our day, as in all times, God has awakened young hearts which have made a profound impression on the entire Catholic world: St. Theresa of the Child Jesus, the greatest Saint of recent times, and her Carmelite sisters, Blessed Elizabeth of the Most Holy Trinity, Teresa of the Andes, and Theresita.

Perhaps even more impressive for a woman living in the world are those virginal individuals who consecrated themselves to God while in the world or were taken home by God even before they had the chance to choose religious life. St. Maria Goretti (1890-1902) stands for the many girls who died rather than lose their virginity. Likewise Karolina Kozka (1898-1914), who spent her short life entirely in the service of her own family and the village parish and at the beginning of World War I was murdered by a Russian soldier when she resisted his attempt to rape her. The Servant of God Edel Quinn (1907-1944) is a fascinating example of a sickly young woman who at the age of twenty consecrated herself entirely to the lay apostolic work of the Legion of Mary; she first cared for the poor in the slums of Dublin for eight years and then worked for seven years as a lay missionary in Kenya and throughout Central Africa, founding hundreds of Legion of Mary groups. She died there in 1944 of tuberculosis.

Finally, here is very recent firsthand testimony from my time in the mission of Gabon: In 1988 a 14-year-old pagan girl named Celia came to the mission. Her father was staunchly opposed to the Church and the Christian faith; he was an animist and quite devoted to the diabolical pagan practices. When he learned that his daughter was preparing for Baptism, he forbade her to come to the mission. She came anyway, secretly supported by her mother. Whenever her father caught her learning the catechism, for example, or coming home from Mass, he beat her, often until she was bloody. Prayer and a growing knowledge of the mysteries of our faith gave Celia the strength to withstand this pressure. The day of her Baptism and First Holy Communion was for her virginal soul the greatest feast day of her life. To outward appearances an ordinary, smiling student, she radiated a great purity. Soon the family moved from the inner city to a town six miles away at the edge of the bush. Consequently she could no longer come as often to the mission as before, which grieved her. Now she had to walk along footpaths for thirty minutes to get to the main road and then ride another thirty minutes by bus. No sooner was she confirmed at age eighteen than she became a catechist for the little girls, whom she loved very much. And so she made her way to the mission three times a week. I can still see her as she used to appear on Wednesday punctually at 3:00 in the afternoon, surrounded by a group of girls; first she would make a visit with them to Our Lord in the Eucharist and then they would disappear into the catechism classroom. We missionaries could find nothing objectionable about her, in particular any of the typical faults of girls such as vanity, envy, or lying.

She experienced one major problem for several years: "I cannot love my father!" she said. She followed with all the more determination our advice to pray for her father whenever she was tempted to think ill of him. Surely it was these prayers that caused the persecution by her father to subside gradually until one day it stopped completely. Even before her Baptism at age fifteen she had joined the girls' youth movement, *Compagnie de l'Immaculée*, and when her family moved from the city she herself founded the group under the patronage of St. Theresa of the Child Jesus for the girls in her neighborhood. Her daily routine was simple: to school in the early morning, at midday back home or to the mission, and several times a week toward evening she gathered the children of the neighborhood and sang and prayed with them and taught them the catechism. Many of them were later baptized by us missionaries.

At the age of seventeen she fell ill with cerebral malaria, a very dangerous disease. Since her mother was a nurse, she was always brought to the hospital at the first signs of an attack and was treated there as well as is possible in Africa. Thanks to this care she lived for another few years. When she was twenty, the attacks became more frequent and more painful, so that she was often bedridden for weeks at a time. Then we brought her Holy Communion—a profoundly moving experience for us missionaries, for seldom had we seen such ardent eyes, such great yearning, such quiet, devoted love! Once when I asked her what she wanted to become in the future, she only said, "To be consumed for HIM like a candle!" Children from the neighborhood came to her sickbed, and as soon as she had regained a little strength, she would pray with them and instruct them. If she didn't have enough strength, her ethereal smile was enough to incite the children to sing and pray. When I said goodbye to her in May of 1994, since I had to leave the mission, she told me: "I would like to offer myself so that our priests might become holy." She died on June 2, 1996, after a true martyrdom of physical pain. Thousands of people came to her burial. About one year after her death her father was converted miraculously and became an exemplary Christian. There are always fresh flowers at her grave, which is extraordinarily rare in Gabon.

What was so attractive about her? Her simplicity, her inner beauty, her radiant, virginal purity, and her love for God and for souls which blossomed forth from it and was preserved even in deep suffering.

What can we say about these great examples? They give us the key to the mystery of virginity: preserving one's energies for eternal, boundless love. After all, the ultimate, greatest, and most sublime destiny of every human being is union with Christ; and for a woman, to be betrothed to Christ. The flower exists for this love, it wants to blossom for Him, and she knows that this blooming will be eternal.

Virgo Virginum Immaculata

The most exalted ideal of virginity, however, is the Immaculata herself, the Virgin of virgins. The Hebraism "virgin of virgins" means that she is not only a virgin in a pre-eminent fashion, but is also the archetype, model, and original pattern of all virginity. She is the source of the beauty of every virgin, the inner mainstay of her harmony and integrity. For when God created the world, "she was there" (cf. Prov. 8:22ff.). As an architect first devises a perfect plan for constructing a building, so God has His masterpiece, the Virgin Mary, before His eyes as the primordial plan, as the flawless *(Immaculata)* original concept *(Conceptio)* of all that is created. Thus she becomes the root, the source, the archetype of all things. All the beauty of creation is like an echo of her beauty. Every perfection of a creature has its measure and pattern in her.

However, because this perfect masterpiece of God is a woman, it follows that of all the creatures that He made, women, and especially virgins, have a special relationship to her, and their most profound destiny consists of becoming, so to speak, rays of this sun, faint images and copies of it. From each of these images proceeds a ray of that primordial plan of God into the dark world, like a final hint of paradise, like a secret gleam of that "new heaven and new earth." This, above all else, is the great duty of woman: to be an image, a living icon of the Immaculata.

That is why it is so necessary for a woman, a virgin, to follow her prototype. Mary gives the example of the virginal life and vocation, and the perfection of feminine nature comes about through conformity to her: to the extent that a woman reflects HER in her life, she becomes precious, strong, pure, and preternaturally beautiful. All the saints have cast themselves into Her Heart like molten material into a mold, and in that way they were formed according to Her example. She encompasses all sanctity within Herself, She is the source of all the most varied forms of virginity, from the most obscure girl who, unknown to the world, performs her service with the utmost modesty, to the most exalted, extraordinary missions of those women who are meant to show the world the strength and power of virginal beauty, such as St. Catherine of Siena or St. Joan of Arc, the Maid of Orleans, or St. Theresa of the Child Jesus.

Thus the Immaculate Virgin is the source of all beauty and harmony that we find in the nature of the *virgo*. This becomes evident in an extraordinary way when She appears on earth. As dissimilar as these appearances are, in every case Mary is there in the overwhelming splendor of Her radiant beauty and youth. No artist can reproduce the harmony of her countenance as it appeared on the *tilma* [cloak] of the visionary [St.] Juan Diego during Her appearance in 1531 on Tepeyac Hill in Mexico as Our Lady of Guadalupe. The shepherd children of Fatima described Her as being "all light," and Bernadette testified about the Immaculata at Lourdes that, in comparison to the grace of being able to see Her for just a moment, all the beauties and glories in the world are absolutely nothing and even seem ugly. The visionary at Lourdes also noted the peculiar character of the virginal beauty of the Immaculata: On the one hand She is so heavenly and untouchable that one hardly dares to look up at Her, and on the other hand She is so attractive that one wants to draw as close to Her as possible. That is the most profound mystery of Her spotlessness, which appears here not only in its negative aspect as freedom from all stain of sin, but also as the completely positive privilege of imaging God, of being completely full of the inexhaustible light of the divine Spirit.

When the Church prays to Mary or speaks about Her, she usually uses the magnificent title: *Beata Maria semper Virgo*—the Blessed, ever-Virgin Mary. In doing so she emphasizes the timeless, constant, and perpetual character of Mary's virginity. The word *semper*, therefore, testifies that Her virginity transcends the changing and passing of all earthly things and constitutes a permanent, eternal value. Thus Mary, as the *SEMPER VIRGO*, is privileged to represent in the created order the boundless virginal beauty and the pure, ardent, and infinite love of God in a most sublime fashion. All virginal creatures participate in Her perpetual virginity, and the Church teaches us that in eternal blessedness this participation is a special mark of distinction called the "aureole" or halo: the Virgins, the Martyrs, and the Doctors of the Church will receive a special reward in heaven corresponding to the particularly glorious and outstanding victory that these Christians won here on earth in their fight for the heavenly crown. This very special honor will be bestowed on them because, as St. Thomas teaches, virginity must be won by a long, hard battle which is not inferior to bloody martyrdom.[6] In the well-known vision of St. Maximilian Kolbe, the Immaculata appeared to him when he was ten years old and told him to choose between two crowns: a white one, the symbol of the "martyrdom of virginity," and a red one, the symbol of the "martyrdom of blood."

The "*semper*," the perpetual character of virginity, which is expressed so profoundly in this summons by Mary, leads us finally into the "*semper*," the perpetual character of God's limitless nature; He made creatures so that they might be an imitation, an echo, and a reflected splendor of His own integrity and perfect harmony. If man was created to honor God and to reflect His glory, then this takes place most profoundly and most purely in the mystery of virginity.

Virgo Fidelis

The mystery of virginity is deeply connected also with fidelity to God, trust in God, faith in God. On earth Mary lived out her virginal dedication primarily through her faith. Faith was demanded of her to the limits of what is humanly possible, indeed, beyond those limits: from the very beginning she had to have blind faith in the angel's message that she was to become the Mother of God without losing her virginity. She had to believe that the tiny Child who was born in the stable and laid in the manger was not only the Messiah, but God Himself. She had to believe in His eternal victory even at the moment when He was hanging on the Cross and seemingly suffered His ultimate defeat. She kept the faith in the darkest hour of Good Friday when all the disciples, even the best, were wavering in their faith.

From earliest Christian times this strong faith that nothing can disturb, that cannot be tainted by the smallest speck of doubt, has been called "virginal faith." And this is one element of spiritual virginity which precedes physical virginity and actually makes it valuable in the first place. And the Immaculata communicates this same strong, virginal faith especially to virginal souls. Why? Because these people do not dissipate and waste their spiritual energies on the mul-

---

[6] St. Thomas Aquinas, *Summa Theologica*, Supplement, q. 96, art. 11.

tiplicity of earthly desires, but rather save them up for the one thing necessary.

From this perspective one can understand how in times of crisis in the Church, it was always the pure virgin who kept and defended the faith. Thus St. Catherine of Alexandria is the patroness of philosophers: On account of her dazzling beauty the Roman governor tried to dissuade her from the Christian faith through the persuasive powers of his best philosophers and thinkers. She replied to their objections with such wisdom that she converted many of them. In a similar way we see the influence of St. Catherine of Siena and St. Teresa of Avila, who decisively influenced ecclesiastical life. St. Theresa of the Child Jesus was declared the patroness of the missions, although she never left her cloister, because she lived out her faith so heroically and preserved it in virginal purity—so much so that she merited the light of faith for countless souls through her heroic suffering in the dark night of faith. Today, in a time of severe crisis, traditional communities of nuns are the ones who have performed the greatest service to the Church. It is very significant that Archbishop Lefebvre often visited their convents and sought advice from the sisters in charge. "They have preserved the *sensus fidei* (the sense of the faith)," he used to say. Hidden virginal forces are at work, serving all projects for rebuilding and preserving the unadulterated, virginally intact faith; these women religious dedicate themselves entirely to passing on the light of truth to souls and thus maintaining the faith, without which there is no true life or salvation. Although insignificant in the world's eyes, this unassuming band of teachers and educators is great and exalted in God's sight because of their service in the schools, hospitals, and nursing homes, in the print apostolate and the youth movements. Thus as a matter of principle, a faithful virgin is one of the most significant support personnel, for in the midst of a general abandonment of the faith, they receive the special grace of collaborating in an outstanding way "so that the Church might continue to exist."

Sponsa

The most profound element in the mystery of virginity is the total orientation of the virginal heart to God, and therein lies already the intensification of this mystery in the mystery of the mystical espousal. We have noted that the virginal aspect of woman considers her in herself, so to speak, and shows what value she herself represents. When we speak of the combination of two different elements, we must first consider them individually before we put them together. Thus an examination of the virginal aspect is absolutely necessary. It forms the foundation, as it were, on which the entire mission of woman can now be constructed.

We have also noted that woman is always created by God for a Thou; she comes into being second after man, as "flesh of his flesh, bone of his bones" [Genesis 2:23]. He precedes her, but it is not good for him to be alone, for he needs her as the other half of humanity. She, however, needs him as the one to whom she can give and confide all of her inner strength and power to love. Their union can fulfill its mission on earth completely only when man and woman unite in a single flame of love and thus return to God from whom they came. This union, however, can take place only if it is based on the order and harmony established by God, to which the unique character of each individual corresponds, whereby the one complements the other in a positive way. Now what does this intertwining look like?

Let us again inquire first about the daily experience in a woman's life: A young girl already experiences family life much more deeply than a boy. It is the feeling of security at home that draws the girl again and again into her parents' house. It is typical for a maturing girl to dream. The legends and tales about the prince who makes the princess happy, about the knight who battles for his lady and wins the victory, were already known in antiquity. The troubadours of the Middle Ages expressed this primordial longing to be a bride in profound lyrical poetry. And then the time comes when her first love stirs for a specific male person, whom she pictures in her imagination as an almost superhuman, perfect ideal. But what takes place in the girl's heart with respect to this beloved ideal image? She wants to be there for him, to cook the finest dishes for him, to put her home in order as nicely as possible for him, and to make herself as attractive and beautiful as she can. And then when he is there, she would like to lean on him and feel that she is protected by him and safe. Finally there is relief from the anxiety that she so often feels when she is alone, as though at the mercy of the forces of darkness and obscurity. This terrible feeling of loneliness vanishes, the sense of isolation and the pain of not being understood and loved by anyone.

Another experience is of a rather religious nature. In our life of faith Christ takes the central place. Now a boy and a girl experience the Person of our Lord Jesus Christ differently. For the boy He is the King, the Lord of the Christian army. For the girl the Fatherhood of God is especially important at first, as we see very clearly in the spirituality of St. Theresa of the Child Jesus and of St. Catherine of Siena. But when Christ becomes central, then the experience of the companion, the friend, the beloved Thou, the Bridegroom predominates. When the young woman meditates on His hidden life, she would like to be His sister or even, like Mary, His mother.

When she meditates on His public life, she is moved by His attitude toward the women who are lovingly devoted to Him, like the Samaritan woman and Mary Magdalen. She would like to sit at His feet like Mary of Bethany or serve Him in practical ways like Martha. Above all, however, the girl is profoundly moved and disturbed at the thought of His bitter suffering: She would like to be present with Veronica and help to soothe His pain. What moves her most of all is Christ's love for her, the way His heart beats and pours out its blood for her heart, the way His blazing eyes look at her as only a husband and wife can look at each other.

These experiences demonstrate sufficiently that a woman is fulfilled by being for a man; after all, that is why God created man as male and female. If we want to examine now this second essential aspect of woman, we must also consider the essentially corresponding and complementary attitude of man, and finally their mutual union, for precisely in this union the partial pictures complete each other in one great image and likeness of God, somewhat like the two sides of a medal. Therefore the following reflections will lead us first into the deeper nature of being a bride and into the duties and obligations that result from it. Above all, however, we will see how man and woman, by fulfilling their complementariness, are an image of the attitude of all creation in its relation to God.

Action and Reaction

The Fathers of the Church like to view the relation between Creator and creation as action and reaction, as departure and return, as creative Word and receptive, echoing answer. God creates all things from nothing; that is His creative deed, His action. The creature responds to this gift with thanks and appreciation; that is its reaction. God creates human beings for eternal happiness and gives them the necessary means of attaining that goal: that is His action. Human beings respond by taking these means and returning to God; that is their reaction.

This polar relation between God and the creature is now represented or symbolized by the polarity of man and woman. Here the man represents God's action: to him is allotted the natural task of building up the world, of organizing, ordering, and governing it, of devising the means whereby everything can fulfill its purpose and attain its goal. That is why he is usually the inventor, builder, artist, lawmaker, leader, and judge.

The world's response to God's action is represented by the woman's attitude: she is the receptive one who receives God's action into herself. She very concretely "con-ceives" the child and carries it for nine months in her womb. To God's challenging word, "I will!" she answers, "Behold, here I am! Let it be done to me according to Thy word!" There are many symbols that depict this attitude: for instance, the rose and the lily which open up to the light of the sun. There is the wide open vessel, the chalice, which reaches up like two outstretched hands full of expectation and longing. Everything calls to her, "Come!" "The Spirit and the Bride say: come!" [Apoc. 22:17]. Therefore to receive the divine life in this way, to be possessed by God, is to be a bride. Concretely a woman will live out this bridal existence in her devotion to a specific Thou, to her husband, to her friend, or in her total, spousal self-donation to Christ.

Woman as bride therefore embodies the return, the flowing back of all creation to God. Through her bridal response, her yes as a reaction to God's loving activity, she stands before everyone as an example, a reminder that life does not consist of that self-seeking which wants to have everything for oneself alone and looks at everything only from the perspective of whether it pleases or is useful to one's own ego. This egotism twists a human being in upon himself, causes him to center everything around himself and to think only about himself.

Pope John Paul II rightly called such a mentality "the culture of death" because this fundamental attitude closes off a human being in barren isolation and makes him incapable of understanding the real meaning of his life as a return to God. Such a person seeks happiness only in himself, in the ego, to which he sacrifices everything in life that is great and truly beautiful—for example a happy family, which exists, after all, only in the self-donation of a father and a mother. Furthermore, the millions of children who are murdered in their mother's womb and the millions of elderly, weak, and sick people who are without assistance are ultimately the result of this egotism.

In contrast, woman as bride proclaims that the meaning of life consists of submerging every hour, every event, every deed in the great movement of returning home to God. Everything must be permeated by the firm resolution, by the great yearning to open oneself up to the boundless ocean of God who pours Himself out so lovingly. She hears Christ's call: "Behold, I stand at the gate and knock" (Apoc. 3:20) and opens wide the gates to Him (Ps. 24).

In the Gospel our Lord Himself describes this mystery of man and woman as the image of active, divine creation and of the receptive, responsive attitude of the creature in the parables of the mustard seed and the leaven (Lk. 13:19ff.). The mustard seed, which at the start is so insignificant yet matures into a large tree in which the birds make their nests, profoundly expresses the working of man, which grows in externally visible making, building, and organizing. His action is aimed at preparing a dwelling place and a livelihood for others, who receive his action and, thanks to it, have a house and home. Immediately afterward, Christ presents the parable of the yeast, which leavens the dough and permeates each part of it. Yeast per se already suggests woman, who does not work outdoors but rather indoors, so as to provide the food that is necessary for life. Moreover a woman works in just this way for the kingdom of God, but quite unlike the man. The yeast is just as important for life as the mustard seed that grows. But we don't see the yeast; it works invisibly, in a hidden, unknown way. And yet it permeates the dough and changes it so that it has the quality that gives it meaning and purpose, namely to become human nourishment. Yeast has neither form nor color nor structure. Someone who knew nothing about its transforming power would not even be able to tell that it exists. In this same way a woman works for the kingdom of God, for the missionary work of evangelizing souls, whether it be in the family, in her neighborhood and circle of acquaintances, or in her spiritual family, the Church, the parish, the school, or various works of charity. Like yeast she permeates everything with her care and her love. She serves God and souls usually in a hidden, unknown, discreet way; she performs all her commonplace daily duties generously and wholeheartedly. And the reaction, the response of creation consists precisely of this guardianship, preservation, and loving reception of the divine action: wasting none of the creative love, but rather accepting it personally as a bride, sacrificing oneself for it so as to maintain it.

Actio *and* Passio—*Giving and Receiving*

Another aspect of spousal reciprocity is the polarity of active and passive, giving and receiving. Thus man in creation represents the active, giving aspect, while woman represents mainly the passive, receptive aspect. He is like a spring; she is the channel, the pool that receives the water and carries it further. He is the shaper; she is the material that allows itself to be shaped. He is the architect and master builder who constructs the building; she is the shrine, which is to say that the woman fills the constructed room with light and life. He provides the seed of new life; she is the womb that receives the life and enables it to grow. He is the unsettled wanderer who spends his day in external work; she is the home that welcomes the weary pilgrim on this earth and allows him to rest beside the warm hearth. He approaches her as the one who desires; she is intent on being desired and possessed by him, as a goblet is filled with precious liquid.

The external signs of this bridal wish to be desired correspond to her natural aptitude to make herself beautiful and attractive. She knows intuitively that only beauty is attractive and pleasing. That explains her interest in jewelry, her personal appearance, and beautiful clothing. Along these lines her hair, above all, has a special significance: it is not just a natural head covering, as it is for a man; because it can be styled, it is particularly suited to expressing a woman's sense of beauty. If a woman exposes the splendor of her hair, she draws attention to herself. If she hides it under a veil, she remains unnoticed.

Priest and Sanctuary

In this aspect of the bridal nature as passive receptivity and being desired, we find a deeper reason why only a man can be a priest and a woman cannot. Of course this is true principally because Christ instituted the priesthood that way, and we do not have the right to question our Lord and Creator about His decisions. After that reason, however, it is mainly because the priest is the active mediator between God and men. A woman, in contrast, is the receptive womb which "keeps all these words of God and ponders them" (cf. Lk. 2:19). In church architecture, therefore, the sanctuary, the space around the altar, is reserved for the man, and the nave for the woman. Just as grace builds on nature, supplements and perfects it, so too the grace of priestly ordination elevates man's nature as the active one who builds, structures, and orders, taking it up into the divine act of building the kingdom of God through the proclamation of the word of God, into the act of new creation through the administration of the sacraments.

Now it is part of man's nature to desire a woman. Isn't this nature somehow violated if he is required to renounce this desire? The answer is found in the indissoluble character of the priesthood.

A man desires a woman and in doing so manifests and represents his own person: he lays his personal talents and qualities at the woman's feet, so to speak, and in that way expresses his desire. Through Holy Orders, however, the man becomes another Christ and loses, as it were, his own personality, or rather directs his desire now completely and indivisibly to the primal source, to God Himself, to the eternal womb of divinity. To the people, however, and to each woman, he no longer represents himself but Christ, who has taken complete possession of him. That is why the Church has decreed that in the greatest moments of his priestly activity we cannot see his face, for instance in the most important parts of Holy Mass or in the confessional. For then his personality steps back and yields completely to Christ as the primary agent. The real attention of the faithful, when they see the priest at the altar or in the confessional, is directed to the eternal High Priest, whom they see through the earthly appearances of His earthly instrument. To help them in this, the Church commands the priest to approach the altar only in liturgical vestments, so as to show even more clearly that it is Christ in the first place who stands before them and offers the sacrifice.

A woman, in contrast, is directed toward a man, and her whole nature is "wanting to be desired," hoping that he will look at her, pay attention to her, and admire her beauty. Consequently the priesthood contradicts her most authentic nature: "to be seen and possessed." Already by her female constitution, her hairstyle (however modest), her figure, and her gestures, she automatically draws attention to herself when she is set in front of others. But if she draws the attention of others to herself, to her person, her body, her voice, and her gestures, then she likewise automatically distracts from Christ. That would be exactly the opposite of what the duty of a priest is.

What, then, is her role in the sacred liturgy? The liturgy is man's most solemn encounter with God; it is the renewal of everything involved in Christ's sacrifice. It is the highest act of divine worship of the Mystical Body of Christ and thus complete union with Christ. Therefore a woman at the liturgy should be a bride with all her powers and with all her soul.

According to her nature she should be "desired and possessed" by Christ. Since by her nature, however, she tends to draw the attention of others to herself instead, when they see her, when they look at her, she will cover herself and conceal in particular all those characteristics that make her especially attractive to the eyes of others. Now the more she covers herself against the sight of creatures, the more she can open herself to the One who should be everything in the sacred liturgy, and the more she will receive His light and His graces. This is how we should understand the saying of St. Paul that a woman should be silent in church, that she should cover her head (cf. I Cor. 14:34 and 11:5-15). He wants to show her how she can be united most intimately with Christ according to her nature. The precepts of the Church regarding how a woman should dress for the liturgy are also rooted in this concern for her deepest possible union with Christ.

The great symbol of woman's mission in the liturgy, however, is the veil covering her hair, which is what makes a woman particularly attractive externally. The veil conceals her beauty, her inner value, from the world, just as the chalice at Mass is veiled until the Offertory. This symbol shows her infinitely precious value which is hidden from the world and from the superficial curiosity of eyes that are unprepared. By veiling herself from creatures, the woman frees and opens her heart to Him, like that of a bride. The powers of her soul, her heart, and her emotions, otherwise poured out all too liberally on limited things, are closed off from them and open interiorly toward the One to whom they can now devote themselves entirely. In this attitude of being concealed the bride can be completely at the disposal of the divine Bridegroom, and in the Host He can take complete possession of her. The veil is not only the common symbol of woman, it is also the special symbol of the bride; and in the liturgy it is, so to speak, her official "vestment," the specific liturgical garb that promotes the one who wears it to a higher order. The chasuble carries the human priest higher, into the Person of Christ. In a similar way the veil carries the woman higher toward the ideal image of her nature as bride of God.

Justice and Love

For us it is inexpressibly difficult to perceive the unity in two such contrasting attributes of God: that in God there is no difference between justice and love, that He is a kindly Father but also a just Lord, Lawgiver, and Judge. Perhaps in no other respect are man and woman in their complementariness[7] so much an image of God, whose all-surpassing love is manifested precisely in His infinite justice.

A man represents God especially in His attribute of justice. His task is to rule and maintain a just order, that is, to give to each his due and to order everything according to its nature. To accomplish this, he needs the talent for organization; he also needs the authority required to defend and ratify order. A man has a sense of objective order, moderation, and limits. The main thing for him is the duty to give an accounting for his activity; only then comes his dedication.

A woman, in contrast, represents God in His attribute of love. Indeed, before all else she wants to love and to devote herself. She does not ask about the why and the wherefore if only she can love and give of herself. This urge to love knows no bounds, like an unending stream that rushes along.

After the Fall this urge easily became her undoing, as the example of Mary Magdalen probably best illustrates. Doesn't Christ Himself say that she loved much? Yet this love found no stability and thus was poured out everywhere and wasted, as when an expensive drink is spilled on the floor and spreads out everywhere and thus goes to waste. The power of love in a woman's heart needs a hand to hold and guide it, to channel, so to speak, the streams of her love into a specific form, structure, and order. She can be a good steward of her love only when she allows her inner wealth of life-giving love and her feelings to flow into an order supervised by the man. She is the heart; he is the

---

[7] *Ineinander.*

head! She is the seat of love; he is the seat of justice! Only in this sense can we speak about the subjection of the woman to the man.

God allows woman to participate intimately in the mysteries of the life which He has created and allows man to share intensely in His will for justice. To that extent the woman receives the moderation of the order willed by God indirectly through the man. And the man receives the fullness of the life wrought by God through the woman. A woman arrives at complete harmony only when she allows the wealth of her feeling and loving to pour into the order that the man stewards; when she is shaped according to the form and the measure that the man has received from God; when she lets the man be head to her heart. Understood in this way, there is nothing offensive or embarrassing or demeaning about the statements by the Apostle Paul in the First Letter to the Corinthians, nor are they merely products of his era. "The head of every man is Christ; the head of a woman is her husband" (I Cor. 11:3). "A man…is the image and glory of God, but woman is the glory of man" (I Cor. 11:7). This means that it is his glory to shape the fullness of being (the sea of her love) according to the measure that he himself has received from God and to build it into that order. The man is a lawgiver; the woman—the receiver of the law, starting with the smallest society, the family, to the most comprehensive society: God's holy Church, in which the highest representation of the lawgiving God belongs exclusively to the man in the exercise of priestly ministry.[8]

Love, and not the official ministry that orders, makes laws, and governs, has been entrusted to the woman; and this facet of her character makes it clear why the priesthood is contrary to the nature of woman. The most sublime actions of the priest are irruptions of God's omnipotence and eternity into time; they infinitely surpass the personality of the priest. That is why the Church demands that he restrain completely his feelings and the personal expression of his piety and—heedless of himself, so to speak—he should perform the prescribed action according to the Church's norms (rubrics). This is pos-

---

[8] Le Fort, *The Eternal Woman*, 33.

sible for him because God has given him instead an affinity for ordering, for law and objectivity.

This is not possible for a woman, because she cannot deny her nature as a loving, feeling heart. If she stood at the altar, she would not be able to control her feelings about the overwhelming experience. We see this often, for example when a nun makes her solemn profession or a bride pronounces her marriage vows. Endless wonder overcomes her heart, in keeping with her nature—so much so that she feels that she must pour out her heart before God in unrestrained love. This is forbidden, however, in ministerial action, for the liturgy is not a presentation of the subjective piety of a human being, however profound it may be; rather it is a divine act which infinitely surpasses man.

If a woman nevertheless, because of Modernist trends, stands at the altar as an extraordinary minister of the Eucharist, a lector, etc., then this does terrible violence to her nature. The self-control required to carry out the liturgy will either drain or deaden her. In order to suppress her tears forcibly, she must harden her loving heart and inwardly distance herself from the exalted liturgical action. But then she herself no longer participates in it and performs her role in it mechanically. Neither was woman created to perform the ministry in the tribunal of the confessional. Her soul is thoroughly inclined to compassion and sympathy with the weak, so that the demands of justice, of maintaining the objective order, would break her heart.

The Bride—Companion of the Man

Now although the bride and bridegroom represent the eternal mysteries of God and His loving deeds in their contrasting characteristics, they do so even more in their union. This union is the prerequisite for motherhood, but in itself it also represents another value. Before she becomes a mother, the bride is the companion of the man. This reveals another aspect of her womanly nature: In their union the two become responsible for each other on their way to God; as her husband's companion the wife participates in his creative mission. The archetype of this companionship is Mary, the New Eve, the *"alma socia Christi,"* the most-pure associate of Christ the Redeemer, who as Co-Redemptrix participates in His theandric [divine-human] work.

We find this companionship even in the natural order as a creative community of life: woman as friend, beloved, co-worker. There are well-known historical examples of the creative collaboration of man and woman as the bride of his intellect, especially in the productive mutual inspiration of Dante and Beatrice, of Michelangelo and Vittoria Colonna, of the poet Hölderlin and Diotima, of Goethe and Frau von Stein, or of Richard Wagner and Mathilde Wesendonk.

What does this bridal companionship actually consist of? Usually it is not an active collaboration with the man's work, but rather her devotion. When it is a question of the union of the two, Sacred Scripture says: "The man knows the woman." This applies not only to their bodily but also to their intellectual and spiritual union. This means that the man recognizes in the woman's devotion the precious thing that she gives away, the stream of life, the guarded treasure, the value of all being, indeed even the supernatural life that God has given to her to guard and to communicate. Man's activity, as we have seen, is the concrete creative momentary building of a visible work. By giving herself to him, the woman presents to him the dimension of the invisible, timeless ocean of the vital fullness of natural and supernatural being and immerses it in his activity. And so his creative activity becomes full of life, sunlight, warmth, sustaining power, and, above all, love.

This brings to light the symbol of the MIRROR: in the devoted bride the man sees his own work and his own nature in its perfection that transcends time. The bride's dowry is the gift that frees man from his loneliness and allows him to grow intellectually and spiritually as well beyond his personal limitations. Not only in the sense that left alone he would not have the strength to carry on and complete what he has begun without the loving presence of his companion, whose smile spurs him on, but also in the sense that through her quiet existence and collaboration he is no longer someone who creates only for himself; instead the great nameless stream of creative life runs through him, making his activity noble, lasting, and worthy of God.

He owes all this to his bride, his companion. In her most exalted perfection, Mary is the "Mirror of Justice." Christ, the Sun of Justice, looks into her heart and finds, as though in a mirror, His own justice, that is, the fullness of His work which justifies man in God's sight. By giving herself to Him, she returns to Him all the fullness that she has received from Him, and thus she presents to Him as though in a mirror His entire work of redemption. And whoever looks into this mirror afterward finds in it everything that God has done for mankind.

We find this creative, spousal collaboration at the highest spiritual level in the great friendships of the saints. What did St. Clare give to St. Francis, or St. Teresa of Avila to St. John of the Cross, or St. Jane Frances de Chantal to St. Francis de Sales, to mention only the most important ones? Would the greatness of the one even be imaginable without the spiritual companionship of the other? This is most evident, however, in the religious communities that arose from their collaboration. The female branches of the Benedictines, Franciscans, Dominicans, Carmelites, etc., make clear this companionship of the bride, who is entirely a bride of Christ, but as such, according to God's will, is connected by spiritual spousal ties with the male branch of the order (usually with the community as such, but now and then with an outstanding representative of that community). She contributes to the inspired work of the founder the quiet warmth and power of life and the ardor of extravagant love. The two together, however, form the totality of the work in God's kingdom.

This can be proved by negative examples: If this spousal tie is broken and the communities are "separated," then both parts become unfruitful. If the man works unilaterally at his projects and excludes the nature and participation of woman, he produces imitations of the Tower of Babel, the names for which [in Latin and other European languages] are all in the masculine gender: liberalism, materialism, socialism, communism, modernism. As he created these mindsets, man felt that he was alone in these fields and hence designed them in the image of his own sex. Where the collaboration of woman (the dispenser of life, the servant of love) is excluded, all that remains is rigid pride, cold indifference, and ultimately death.

"Ecce Ancilla Domini"

How does the bride make a gift of her power to love? How specifically does she live out her creative devotion? She wants to serve; she wants to do something for her beloved. For someone who loves, serving is absolutely necessary. Even the development of all her charm and beauty is not supposed to be for her own sake, but rather a service performed for the beloved Thou. And if thoughts of vanity and selfishness appear, she knows that these are contrary to her intrinsic nature as bride. Although service is an unbearable burden for the egotist, for the lover it is a great joy and profound happiness. In this way love can express itself and become visible in one's concrete work. Service is self-giving put into practice. This is abundantly clear in the "Bride of the Lamb": the Queen of heaven and earth, the Mother of the Most High, knows only one attitude toward Him: "Behold the handmaid of the Lord."

Divine Providence desired that Our Lady's bridal nature be directed initially toward a man to whom she was betrothed, and according to St. Thomas this constituted a real marital bond. How did Mary live out her betrothal with Joseph? In total service. She concealed herself from the world to the point of complete obscurity. Only he knew anything about her secret, although not everything by far. But this knowledge was enough for him to take his place as her guardian and mainstay. She, in turn, gave him her love completely, was there for him totally, and served him in everything. Her whole life until her Assumption looks no different: Egypt, Nazareth, accompanying Jesus in His public life even to the Cross—it was one single uninterrupted service. But this service was permeated, motivated, and caused by her ardent bridal love, which cannot think of herself but only of the beloved THOU.

This is also the basic theme of the Canticle of Canticles in Sacred Scripture: The bride does not rest, but instead searches ceaselessly until she finds her beloved. There is no espousal without this seeking, without this great yearning for union, without painful longing for the beloved. As soon as the beloved is present, however, the bride surrounds him with care and service.

We see this, finally, in the great brides of God who preserved their beauty for the divine Bridegroom whom they loved above all else. Here it becomes particularly evident that this service is not only an activity concerned about the physical well-being of the beloved, as in the case of Martha, but that it is also a quiet "sitting at his feet," as exemplified by Mary of Bethany, who "chose the best part." In the most profound sense, service is being there for the other, with heart and soul and body, as St. Agnes expressed it so beautifully: "To Him alone I remain loyal; to Him I commend myself with complete devotion. What I desired I already see; what I hoped for I already possess. I am wedded in heaven to Him whom I loved solely on earth."[9]

Mater

"You did not choose me, but I chose you and appointed you that you should go and bear fruit and that your fruit should abide" (Jn. 15:16). These words of Jesus to His apostles apply also in an extended sense to everyone, for every human being has been chosen by Christ and destined to develop, through his free initiative, the aptitudes that have been given to him and thus to reach his perfection. This development of one's original gifts is what is meant by "bearing fruit," the free co-operation of the human being with God's grace, the life of love in word and deed. This is the meaning of the parable of the talents as well. We have received natural and supernatural aptitudes as a gift from God and now have the task of developing and increasing them. Someone who buries them instead and does not use them to do the work that God has assigned him will be severely punished.

This fruitfulness is so important, therefore, because it is proof that we take God seriously. The grain of wheat, symbol of His love, has fallen on the soil of our good will, and we direct our lives toward Him, so as to live according to His will. The honest effort to do so al-

---

[9] Responsories at Matins for the Feast of St. Agnes.

ready causes the grain of wheat to sprout and promises a magnificent yield. If a small act of love of neighbor—for instance, giving one's neighbor a glass of water for love of God—produces fruits for eternity and is rewarded by God, how fruitful will a whole life be that is spent striving to carry out God's mission! And this very fruitfulness will be the hallmark of the true Christian: "By this all men will know that you are My disciples, if you have love for one another" (Jn. 13:35). "You will know them by their fruits" (Mt. 7:16).

For the woman this means that her virginal being, namely the integrity and harmony of her soul and heart and body, must likewise bear fruit. Similarly her bridal existence is not the ultimate good; the gift of self to the beloved THOU is likewise supposed to bear fruit. This fruitfulness is for her, finally, the full development of her nature, and therein she attains the fullness of womanhood, her perfection, her sanctity.

Now what is the fruit of the union of a man and a woman, the outward expression of their love? A child! Indeed, true love is not just emotional, a stirring of one's feelings and heart that wishes the beloved well, but it is also effective: it proves itself in concrete action, in the sacrifice of one's own will, in the acceptance of the God-given task of bearing fruit.

Now what is this task of woman which is her mission on earth, the ultimate reason why she is a virgin and bride? Everything leads up to motherhood. The very structure of a woman's body and her peculiar psychological and physiological nature prove that she is designed to be a mother.

This is demonstrated also by the basic experiences of being a woman, among which love for children is quite obvious. Moreover as a rule a woman has a much better sense than a man for specific details, for the little everyday things, since raising a child takes place precisely in the specific everyday events, in the little hidden details that must not be overlooked. Otherwise the child's education would be neglected. Thus the woman is much more at home in everyday family life than among the big ideas of politics and business. Thus a penchant for keeping a house in order, for preparing meals and a thousand little everyday things is mainly characteristic of a woman.

This maternal instinct comes to the fore in a little girl when she carries her little brother or sister around, dresses dolls and behaves like a mother toward them. As a girl grows up she dreams of a beloved home of her own, surrounded by many children to whom she gives life. This ordering of the woman to the child as its mother comes to light in an extraordinary way, however, when her own little child looks at its mother and smiles at her. Then the mother knows that in this moment she is, so to speak, everything for the child and that she also wants to be everything for the child.

Physical and Spiritual Motherhood

Just as a human being per se has a natural and a supernatural life, so too a woman is initially inclined to motherhood in her natural life, with all the powers of her body, her heart, and her soul. Thus the first woman was named Eve, the life-giver. A mother bears new life, gives life to the child, guards and looks after it, nourishes and raises it.

Above and beyond this, however, there is also a spiritual motherhood, which already begins within physical motherhood. In fact true child-rearing is not just concern for the child's bodily welfare and the development of its natural capabilities, but also the awakening and sustaining of the child's supernatural life. This spiritual motherhood or care for supernatural life is just as superior to physical motherhood as the soul is to the body, as eternal life is to life in this world. Every true mother is also the spiritual mother of her children, although she is absorbed to a great extent by the physical, earthly side of her maternity.

That is why the Church also needs women who devote themselves wholly and entirely to spiritual motherhood, for it is much more difficult, arduous, and demanding to maintain and protect spiritual life than physical life. Moreover, there are also the failures of women caused by sin, which are particularly evident in their neglect to pass on the supernatural life. Although it is easy to bring children into the world, it is difficult to rear them also in keeping with their supernatural destiny.

All these facts show the necessity of spiritual motherhood in order to pass on life really and in its fullness. The woman who devotes herself to this, her greatest goal in life, can do it in religious life, where she exercises this motherhood directly in an active religious community, or indirectly in a contemplative cloister. She does this in the world also, though, whenever and wherever she devotes herself to the protection, nourishment, and support of life, whether as a teacher and spiritual mother in a school, or in caring for sick and elderly people.

The Mother's Heart

The family is the cell of society. If the family is sick, then so is society with all its members. If the family is ruined, then so is society with all its members. And today that is largely the case.

Again and again in his addresses to young married people, Pope Pius XII emphasized that the wife is the sun of the family. As the sun emits its rays, as a candle is consumed, so a mother is consumed for the sake of her family. It depends on her whether the atmosphere in the family is filled with the light of cheerful devotion, with the clean, warm, healthy air in which delicate plants like her children can grow. From this follows an essential task for the woman: Nowhere does a woman develop the full scope of her mission so much as in the family circle. The family needs a structure; it is a living organism with head and heart and members. If the order is disrupted, the family suffers, withers, and may even be entirely ruined.

The atmosphere of the family, its vital pulse, is love. In this soil new life is conceived, born, nourished; here alone do the plants thrive. That is why the woman has the decisive role in the family. If the man fails to meet his responsibilities, that is bad, but nothing is lost yet. If the mother fails, as a rule the family is destroyed, unless by a miracle God preserves it (which often happens especially today, because God sees the chaos in which people live and has infinite compassion for us).

How often a pastor is deeply upset by the almost insurmountable problems of today's youth, which almost always result from a lack of light, protection, and warmth, which the mother is obliged to give to her children. But the contrary is true also: what a joy to find families everywhere in which the shining eyes of children and the fresh faces of young people testify to the devotion and care of the parents.

The deeper reason lies in the fact that the woman, through her voluntary subordination, her love and self-sacrifice, sets for all the others an example of the attitudes that are necessary for the very existence of society. When everyone wants to rule, a society breaks up. Only from a mother do the children learn the necessary attitudes on which every society is built: submission, obedience, love. For this reason God gave her a deep affinity for the weak and helpless. Therefore one of her characteristics is genuine sympathy, compassion on human misery, kindness to those who are sad or have experienced failure.

Since she is the dispenser, steward, and servant of life, already by this natural inclination she creates a close bond among all those to whom she has the privilege of transmitting life, whether naturally or supernaturally. Most importantly, however, through this transmission of life, which after all comes from God, she creates a bond between her loved ones and God. She is truly the heart of the family.

This is why a girl has to prepare for her mission while she is still growing up. In the family the older sister has the duty of standing beside her mother and substituting for her as needed. In preparing for adulthood, a young woman should thoroughly ponder the problems of family life and acquire some knowledge of the principles of child-rearing. Only then will she be a good mother, the sun of her family, the source of light and life.

The Divine Maternity as the Prototype of All Motherhood

All motherhood comes from the Mother of all mothers. The Immaculate Mother of God is the model for every mother; her motherhood is the ideal, the basis, the heart, and the goal of all creaturely motherhood. Here in a surprising new way the nature of woman proves once again to be the expression and image of God on earth. The polarity and complementariness of man and woman mentioned at the beginning, which in the interdependence of their different and often opposite characteristics reflects the all-encompassing Oneness of God, appears here in the special relation of mother and child. This is probably the most intimate relationship that there can ever be between human beings.

In this sense Mary's Divine Maternity is the most perfect creaturely image and manifestation of the most intimate relation between Father and Son within the Most Holy Trinity. In Mary this is at the same time a spiritual and a bodily reality: bodily, since she is the physical mother of God, and Christ is flesh of her flesh, blood of her blood; spiritually, since she conceived Him "first in her heart and then in her body" *(prius in mente quam in corpore)*. Thus in her own motherhood she becomes the prototype and ideal of all bodily and spiritual motherhood. If God Himself defines the most intimate possible relationship between Himself and a creature as the relation between mother and child, then we can say that all earthly motherhood finds its deepest meaning in connection with the Divine Maternity. Mary's motherhood is the model and standard of every sort of motherhood on earth, and every instance of motherhood on earth is meant to be an echo of the Divine Maternity. That means that the mother (and by analogy the father also) experiences her motherhood fully when she views it in light of Mary's motherhood.

The parents see their child as a gift from God; they see in the child the presence of the Child Jesus. Conceiving the child and carrying it in the womb becomes for the mother a living reminder and "representation" of the conception of the Eternal Word and of carrying Jesus Christ in one's heart. The birth and the raising of the child are understood as symbolic of the divine mission, that is, the sending forth of Jesus Christ into the world and His proclamation which gives birth to Christ in souls. Jesus Himself confirms this way of looking at it when He says that whoever does His will is "brother, sister and mother" to Him (Mt. 12:50).

Mary's Divine Maternity makes comprehensible to the Christian, and in particular to the Christian woman, the mission that she has to fulfill in her short life. We have to continue the mission of the Son in the world, to be His instruments to help lead people home to Him, to prepare the way for the sake of their eternal happiness. This is nothing less than a spiritual fatherhood or motherhood with respect to souls, which in a certain way become our children. How do they become our children? Through our prayers and sacrifices, our example, and the dedication of our lives, we impart Christ to them, communicate the grace of Christ to them, and act as instruments of the Immaculata, so that she can bear Christ in their souls: and that, of course, is her Divine Maternity. "What do you want me to do?" each one of us must ask God. The answer is always: "Be a father or mother of souls! Imitate the motherhood of My Mother in your life."

The meaning of spiritual motherhood goes still further, however. In imitating the Mother of all mothers, a woman finds a special relationship to Christ Himself, who wishes to be visible here on earth as a "small and insignificant" child. That is why He conceals Himself also under the unassuming appearances of bread and wine. And He wants us to love Him as Mary loved Him, as a mother loves her child, for there is no more intimate loving relationship on earth than the one between mother and child. Naturally this does not mean the purely natural, physical bond and certainly not the kind of motherhood that has been distorted by original sin and is often full of egotistical needs. This "maternal character" of our relationship to Christ is a compliance with Mary's being, and it is guided by her maternity. But in what way was she the mother of the eternal Son? How did she raise Him, live with Him, speak with Him? Surely the most profound reverence for His majesty was combined with the deepest possible intimacy of her immaculate love. And so that this might not be something abstract and unreal for us, God gives us a very realistic analogy that is experienced intensely.

The most sublime experience in human life is being a father or a mother. Motherhood in its most profound fulfillment leads to the deepest union with Christ.

Finally, this "participation" in the Divine Maternity and living according to its principles leads us to a correct understanding of the presence of God within us: the true mother lives completely for her child, is utterly devoted to it, sacrifices herself for the child. Now, however, this precious jewel is God Himself, the Incarnate Word. Profound reticence, sacred silence and the most intense recollection characterize Mary's relationship to Jesus. Thus her Divine Maternity teaches us something that has been almost entirely lost in our noisy times: prayer in silence and recollection, living in the presence of God. It has become unspeakably difficult for us to be quiet. Modern man flees from silence and can no longer keep silent. Even a spiritual person finds it difficult to maintain an inner tranquility, so turbulent and noisy are the stirrings in his heart. Now, though, he welcomes into his heart the great mystery; something takes place within him as on the day of the Annunciation: God comes into his soul. He can now cherish this mystery and carry it within him, as an expectant mother carries her child within her. However, since God lives within us and bestows upon us His eternal light in indescribable silence, the mother must become very quiet and respect the presence of the Divine Child within her in profound, adoring silence. Mary's Divine Maternity becomes the "model" for our life with God. For a woman who experiences her motherhood in its profound symbolic significance as the expression and realization of God's coming to earth as a Child, her maternity itself becomes a straight path to perfection.

Mother of Mercy

Why is a mother's heart so full of mercy? Why does she have such a deep affinity for the weak and suffering? Here, too, Mary gives us the most profound answer; after all, she is called the "Mother of Mercy." St. Maximilian Kolbe writes about this, the most beautiful title of the Immaculata:

> If someone falls into sin, goes far astray in a life of vice, despises God's graces, no longer looks to the good example of others, no longer heeds salutary inspirations and thus makes himself unworthy of further graces—must such a human being despair? No, not at all!

After all, God gave him a Mother who observes with a sympathetic heart each one of his deeds, every word, every thought. She does not look to see whether he is worthy of grace and love. She is only the Mother of Mercy, and therefore she hastens, even unbidden, to the place where the greatest misery prevails in souls. For if only she comes into a soul, no matter how miserable and soiled with sins and vices it may be, then she does not permit that soul to be lost, but rather begs for it the grace of light for the understanding and the grace of strength for the will, so that the soul might return to its senses and arise from its sins. As the Mediatrix of all Graces she is not only able and willing to grant the grace of conversion from time to time, here and there, but she desires to bring all souls to rebirth.[10]

Imagine a child who has been very bad and wicked, perhaps has committed many crimes and is rejected by the whole world: would his mother, if she is a good mother, ever disown this child of hers? Wouldn't she beg God her whole life long, like St. Monica, for his conversion? And at the slightest sign of remorse in her child, wouldn't she hurry to him and demonstrate her maternal love? And if the child in his despair called "Mother," could her heart ever manage to remain deaf to such a cry for help? Who would ever be afraid to go to his mother?

Here, though, we have not just any mother, but the best of all mothers, whose entire nature is to be the Mother of Mercy. Obviously God wished to give this, His most beautiful and magnificent attribute as "Father of Mercy," to all motherly women, first and foremost, though, to the Immaculata. In order to understand this, we must consider what Divine Mercy is in the most profound sense: namely, God's loving condescension to the little, insignificant ones, to our nothingness, to our essential weakness, and (after the Fall) to our misery. God wants to show the world His Mercy. This mercy is one of God's many attributes, and therefore it is not possible for us to observe it in its pure and simple form. God is mercy, but not only mercy: He is also justice, infinite holiness, etc. Christ, too, who reveals this Divine Mercy in an

---

[10] *Rycerz Niepokalanej* 4 (1925): 131, quoted in O. Domański, *Co dzień ze św. Maksymilianem* (Niepokalanów, 1994), 51.

unfathomable way to the world, even unto death on the Cross, reveals the other divine attributes also: He is, for example, the Judge who rewards good and punishes evil. God, however, wants to show mercy in its pure form as Mercy alone, and therefore He creates a creature in which His mercy is incarnate, so to speak, which in every fiber of its being is Mercy alone: Mary. She herself is the most beautiful work of Divine Mercy: "He hath regarded the humility of His handmaid," and His Mercy spared her from the stain of original sin. God created Mary to be wholly and radically pure; He wishes her to be the object of His Mercy, pre-eminently and absolutely, so that through Mary we might have a share in this Mercy. Her whole being is the personification of the Holy Spirit, the personal LOVE of the Trinity. This Love, however, is manifested to fallen creatures as boundless Mercy which desires to save, heal, lift up, and redeem. Therefore Mary is among human beings the Mercy of God itself. This is taught explicitly by St. Albert the Great. He even says that the name "Queen of Mercy" is the most fitting title for Mary's dignity, and that these titles, "Mother of Mercy" and "Queen of Mercy," belong to no one else.[11]

Now every woman receives a ray from this original plan of God to image forth His attribute of merciful love utterly and entirely in Mary. By entering into this stream of the merciful Heart of Mary and thus bending to care for souls, a woman is already their spiritual mother, a dispenser and sustainer of life, who does not break the bruised reed or quench the smoldering wick, but rather awakens it into a living flame.

Mother of Divine Grace

Now if Mary is solicitous about the lost, the suffering, and the sick, how much more will she be a dispenser of life for the souls in which the life of charity is flourishing. Here she can develop her maternity fully, perpetually dispense supernatural life anew, and be the Mediatrix of all Graces. If Mary, the New Eve, stands beside the New Adam as His companion and, though dependent on Him, nonethe-

---

[11] *Mariale,* q. 75, p. 131, cited in *Ego Sapientia: La Sagesse qui est Marie* (Laval, 1943), 171-172.

less participates fully with Him in the redemption of the world, then it is fitting also that she should give to the world the fruits of redemption, the graces that Christ has won for us, like a mother who is privileged to give life to her child. Spiritual motherhood in general is based on the fact that Christ is the Head and we are the members of His Mystical Body. Mary, however, is Mother of the whole Christ: The same Mother cannot bear the Head without the members, nor the members without the Head; otherwise it would be a monster. In the same way the Head and members are born of the same Mother in the order of grace.[12] Under the Cross, amidst a thousand pains, Mary, through her union with the New Adam and through her cooperation in His redemptive work, brings forth children of God to the life of grace. The fruits of redemption come to us only through her.

Perhaps it is one of the most profound things about the nature and mission of woman that she is privileged to participate in this sublime mystery of the transmission of divine life. In Mary and as a continuation of her, so to speak, a woman is supposed to be mother of divine grace. And for this she needs only to enter into Mary's sentiments and to perform her simple daily duties with a heart burning with love, as she did in Nazareth. She should stand with her under the Cross and suffer silently with that pain and sorrow and thus, through a thousand little sacrifices, bear Christ in souls. That is why a mother in particular needs to be close to the Blessed Sacrament and is drawn almost instinctively to the Holy Sacrifice of the Mass. She not only knows that she will find there the source of all the strength she needs for her life, but senses also that that is the most appropriate place for her: with Mary under the Cross, being the mother of eternal life in souls.

Icona Immaculatae

Mary accomplishes the whole mystery of woman in her tri-une fullness: She is simultaneously and with utter perfection *Virgo*,

---

[12] St. Louis Marie Grignion de Montfort, *True Devotion to Mary*, paragraph 32.

Sponsa, and *Mater*. The Litany of Loreto to the Mother of God expresses this very beautifully through its threefold division of the invocations, albeit in reverse order: first her Motherhood, then her Virginity, and finally the various aspects of her Spousal character, including her royal title as well.

The highest ideal and goal of woman consists of becoming a true image, a perfect icon of the Immaculata. Now our earthly existence is always only a partial, rudimentary effort, as St. Paul says so beautifully (I Cor. 13:9), and that is why even a woman here below can image the mystery of the Immaculata only partially, in a fragmentary way. As a rule one essential attribute appears after the other: childhood and youth are spent in the virginal state, while the young adult woman allows her spousal qualities in particular to burst forth, and the mature woman realizes her nature in her motherhood. Not until old age do these three aspects gradually converge again, but only if the woman during any given phase of her life preserves its proper character like a precious treasure, or—as in Christ's parable—like a talent and has beautified and perfected herself in the spiritual combat. Thus, after the children are grown up, one often sees in good mothers of families a discreet longing re-emerge for a virginal way of life, for a spousal relationship with Christ. But even the marital love of aging parents returns to the ideal of virginity, of spousal self-donation as friendship, as a spiritual union of two burning loves that flare up to God, to the Bridegroom of the soul, Christ.

Now this is also the plan of sanctity for every woman: She only needs to preserve these fundamental attitudes in her soul and to try to shape each day and every hour accordingly while constantly looking to the Immaculata. In that way she will become more and more Her icon, Her living image, an expression of Her on earth.

Just as the priest is a continuation of Jesus Christ in space and time, so too a woman who loves God is a continuation of Mary in space and time. And in this way souls are gained for heaven. For just as the New Adam, Christ, our Redeemer, willed to save the world only in union with the New Eve, Mary, the Co-Redemptrix, so too He continues His redemptive work on earth in His instruments and images: among men in a special way in a priest, who is an image of Christ, and among women especially in the Bride of Christ, the icon of the Immaculata.

In eternity, however, she will be privileged to share in the complete mystery of woman, for then there will be no more husband and wife, but we will be like the angels. Utterly and entirely glorified in Mary, she will be capable of being perfectly *VIRGO, SPONSA, MATER*. Immaculate like her, in ineffable beauty of soul and in glorified love, perfectly pure and holy *(VIRGO)*, completely and utterly united with the divine BELOVED and, in Him and through Him and with Him, with all those whom she has loved with true love *(SPONSA)*, while enjoying the eternal fruits of love *(MATER)*, surrounded by the many children for whom she not only was a dispenser of life on earth, but also is privileged to remain one in eternity: and so God will be all in all.

Specific Consequences

Attire and Outward Comportment

The human body is not something incidental like a cloak, but rather is an essential component of the human being. Through his body a human being expresses himself and manifests the movements of his heart, the thoughts of his mind. Miming and gesturing are more than mere muscular movements; they are part of human language. Clothing, however, is ordered to the body; it conceals and reveals it at the same time. Consequently clothing is likewise an expression, a visible side of the invisible depths of a human being. Therefore everything that we have said about woman must be expressed somehow in the manner in which she presents herself outwardly: in the way she treats her body, in her comportment, in her gestures and words, in her clothing.

A woman's outward behavior and self-presentation is fundamentally different from a man's: her voice, her choice of words, her way of walking, standing and addressing others, and even her clothing, which any department store amply demonstrates. In order to get an in-depth understanding of all these manners of everyday life, we must return to the symbolic character described at the beginning of this book.

We noted that within creation (that is, among the many species of living things) man represents striving upward to the goal, toward "God over us." Now the limbs that carry out this motion [along this journey] are his legs. If these become markedly evident through his clothing (for example if he wears trousers), then this is meant to display precisely this special natural characteristic of a man, for whom it is appropriate to strive toward a goal and thus to move and to bring everything around him into motion so as to realize an idea, to plan and build a structure, to have an effect on the world and to set it in motion.

In contrast, a woman in creation represents the element of rest, or interiority, of "God in us." In order to testify to this outwardly, the limbs by which she moves are hidden; one usually does not see her legs. Thus her skirt or her dress emphasizes her character of stability, the tranquil side of the male-female polarity, her role as foundation and preserver of life. Conversely, when a woman bares her legs, she loses her awareness of her nature and also does not allow others to perceive her nature. Therefore wearing trousers is for a woman an objective denial or at least an ignorance of her characteristics as a preserving, peaceful force, a protective womb. Indeed, what is most lacking in today's world? This restless, inconstant, unstable world that is tossed about in a thousand contrary directions sorely needs a firm support, peace, stability, a home and a hearth to which a person can run and hide and rest and find himself again and renew his strength. But therein lies the authentic mission of woman!

A second symbolic value of clothing is that it covers the body. What we said about the veil is true also in an extended sense for the covering of the whole body. A woman preserves the divine depth of love and life. Thus the greatest mystery of God is entrusted to her heart. One keeps a mystery hidden, though, and does not reveal it; otherwise one would betray it. Similarly a woman betrays the mystery of her nature, which finds expression precisely through the symbolism of the body, when she wears indecent clothing. By baring herself and growing accustomed to being bare, a woman not only endangers her own purity and the purity of those who look at her curiously, but also loses her connection to her own depths, to her most authentic mystery. Her nature then becomes flat, empty, banal, and incapable of fulfilling her mission well.

There is another aspect to this: Something that is precious is hidden from the world and concealed from indiscreet eyes. Clothing covers the beauty of a woman's body, her grace, her charm, her nature as "wanting to be desired." That is precisely what is precious about her and comparable to a wonderfully beautiful flower or a golden chalice.

A woman has received this attractiveness in order to save it, as a bride, for her beloved Thou, the bridegroom, to whom she reveals herself entirely and gives all her womanly charms. For him she saves her beauty and, in marriage, those members of her body which make her especially desirable to a man. If she reveals and exposes them to the world, it is as though she cast off precious pearls, and she loses the greatest power of her nature: the power to love. Then perhaps her exterior will be desired by many men, but merely as a thing, as an object of lust, and not as a symbol or expression of herself, of her heart. And if she exposes herself in this way to many men, then she is playing with her body as though with a thing, a means of attraction which goes through many hands, and what happens to her then is similar to what happens to a beautiful flower when it goes through many hands and is admired for a moment, but through this handling loses its freshness and quickly withers. Furthermore through this superficial admiration of many observers the flower loses its genuine symbolic force; for after all it is supposed to be the very personal expression of the devotion and love of the giver for the one recipient. Similarly a woman who exposes her charms to many men becomes incapable of giving herself, for one cannot divide up her heart into many parts, and therefore she really gives herself to no one, but only gives her body as an object; her heart, however, remains alone and lonely. For those who see her in that way, uncovered and exposed, do not really desire the woman herself, but instead are seeking in her what will satisfy their own lust.

Finally, clothing also expresses outwardly the state of life which the woman is presently experiencing and to which she is committed. Before she enters the spousal state, a virgin is still free, that is to say, she has not yet chosen her Thou. That is why her clothing, too, and her outward comportment are still rather revealing; this means that within the bounds of discretion and modesty she can display certain charms, a freedom that is often expressed in the splendid colors and elegance of her clothing, in her hairstyle and choice of jewelry. On the other hand she will jealously guard her purity and virginity, will never expose herself indiscreetly or dress immodestly.

As a spouse, though, she has found the beloved Thou to whom she reveals herself entirely, which also entails to some degree shutting herself off from the outside world. Accordingly, she will make an effort not to draw the attention of other men to herself because she does not want anyone to desire her except the man to whom she belongs. She expresses this in her clothing and comportment also, which outwardly is all the more restrained the more intimately involved she is with the beloved Thou. Therefore she will display all of her charms to her husband while concealing them from the world. This restraint and self-concealment concerns not only the body but also the soul. "Behaving oneself" implies this too: Just as a woman can uncover and expose her body, so also can she reveal the life of her soul. Sometimes a young woman basically has only one fault, extreme indiscretion, so that she is always ready to tell people everything about her personal circumstances and feelings. She constantly talks to those around her, whether close friends or strangers, about whatever she happens to be experiencing: whether she is cold or warm, hungry or thirsty, in a good or a bad mood. Finally she ends up revealing her erotic feelings and experiences to anyone who will listen. This sort of self-betrayal is quite common nowadays; indeed, the women's magazines are full of it. In the religious sphere, the charismatic movement, which places a premium on subjective feelings and maintains that they are the working of the Holy Spirit, is to blame for this spiritual exposure of women.

Finally, as a mother she must also consider the example that she gives to her children. The child imitates its mother and is introduced by the mother into the basic realities of being a man or a woman. This often requires of the mother even greater discretion in her clothing and presentation of herself, even and especially in her own home.

Woman as Home-Maker

The original home of a creature is God. God is perfect rest, eternal peace, the destination, ultimate security. A priest, God's representative on earth, despite his missionary activity of conquering the world for God, must dwell completely in God's rest [Psalm 95:11]; he must impress on people this final security in God. Therefore he wears a cassock or soutane, which is not only a symbol of detachment from the world and worldly things, but also similarly to woman's clothing covers the whole body and makes him so representative of God's eternal peace and unchanging happiness on earth.

We have seen that a woman is by nature a guardian of life: She bears life, brings it forth, protects and nourishes it. She is like the good soil or "mother earth" in which plants can flourish. She is the home, the phase of rest, the place of peace, the strong foundation, the root, and as such she represents God's activity in the world, for He is a God of peace, constancy, rest, and security.

We know all too well that our world, apart from its many other negative qualities, has become a world of unrest, of constant change at dizzying speed. It suffers from a permanent nervous disorder, with all its devastating consequences: rudeness, lack of self-control, domineering tendencies, and an inordinate desire for experiences. Yet life can mature, develop, and unfold harmoniously only in an atmosphere of peace, security, and quiet—in other words, at home. If parents communicate to a child nothing but inconstant back-and-forth, unrest, agitation, noise and unease, then something fundamental in his life is disturbed. The little child cries inconsolably when its sleep is disturbed or when it is tired but is not put to bed.

Thus a woman in this world has the special task of being, on the contrary, a source of peace and rest. One of the most beautiful and fortunate things a human being can experience is the assurance that he has a home, a place where he can rest and withdraw from the commotion of everyday cares and concerns and renew his strength and vitality. And that is the woman's role. That is why God, as we have already observed, designed her to have the qualities of constancy, "inertia," patience, and endurance. Constant change is not in her nature. On the contrary, she likes to be at home, beside her own hearth. She is not simply a place of rest; she actively opposes the agitation and unrest of the world, takes it into herself, so to speak, and thus causes it to come to rest. So it often happens that a child comes back home excited, worn out, upset, trembling, and heavy-hearted. The child throws its arms around the mother's neck, perhaps has a good cry and commends itself to her care, and then after a few moments his heart is peaceful and calm again. How indescribably important the restful, imperturbable qualities of a wife are for the husband, too, in his struggle to make a living today. This composure that soothes and radiates peace, this poise when everyone else is losing his temper—that is the great mission of woman in our time, which she can accomplish, however, only if she draws strength from the source of all peace, when she herself comes to rest at the feet of Him who is everyone's final home.

So it is understandable that God tied woman by her very nature to the house. In many places and many countries the mother goes out only to church or to go shopping; otherwise she stays at home. How often, then, the children feel the urge to go back to the house, to their mother who is waiting for them at home, where they can calm down again. The mother at home is the symbol of the strong woman, as described in powerful terms in Sacred Scripture (Prov. 31). In our time, which has seen an almost complete loss of eternal and lasting values, it is the woman who because of her most authentic nature has the mission of maintaining those values and handing them on. She is the place of rest; she carries what is precious within herself and therefore cannot miss out on her vocation by running around, but instead is immobile. A woman carrying her unborn child will often be immobile for months. Her very body is the first home of her child. The same is true of her spiritual constitution: A woman is in complete possession of her home; where she has come to be at home, she feels secure and wants to stay. She is suspicious of everything strange, different, and new. That is why she senses much sooner than a man the danger and threat that is concealed in everything strange. The man, after all, is the discoverer; he enjoys anything new and often loses himself in it. The woman is instinctively on the defense against what is new and immediately asks about the why and wherefore. I am happy in my home, and so what good is something new to me?

This is true at the highest level about the preservation of eternal values, about the transmission of eternal, divine life. Thus the woman has taken all these divine things in and treasured them in her heart. She has become convinced of God's infinite love, the truth of His words, His devotion unto death on the Cross, the graces and means of attaining holiness which Christ has given us in the Church. Now suddenly something new and earth-shaking comes along. Who have always been the first to stand up and "not go along with it"? The women! They were the first to sense that the novelty was destructive, that it undermined true love and true devotion, that it destroyed supernatural life. Books could be written about the mothers in the Catholic tradition, especially about the mothers of priests, who in many, many cases set their sons on the right path precisely through their consistent Catholic motherhood. Thus we arrive for the second time at the conclusion that Catholic Tradition is maintained above all by women.

Woman's Mission in Serving, Suffering, and Hoping

In keeping with her nature and mission in the world, a woman has a special capacity to affirm service; in keeping with her strength to endure, she has a special ability to affirm suffering; and in keeping with her close dependence on God, she has a special gift for preserving hope and trust. Indeed, her whole nature is a service to life, and every impulse of a woman to receive life, to bear it, bring it forth and nourish it, is nothing else than service. True love desires to devote itself to the beloved, and the expression of this devotion is service: to be there for the other, to make his life easier, to make him happy, to do good for him. A human being who truly loves wants to express his love and therefore does not tire of rendering services small and great to the beloved as a proof of his devotion, of his firm resolution: "You are more important to me than anything else in the world. Your welfare and happiness are my greatest happiness." Love says: "It is good that you exist!"

Love desires the greatest good for the beloved and intends to help him attain it. This help, this being-for-each-other is nothing other than the will to serve the other, whereby each one serves the other according to the specific characteristics of his or her sexual nature. The man serves by guiding, leading, creating order and structure. The woman serves life, devotes herself by helping in all ways to dispense, maintain, and renew life. Therefore the more the woman devotes herself to serving life, the more perfect, noble, and beautiful she is. For through Christ service has become the authentic kingly act, the expression of perfect love: "The Son of man came not to be served but to serve, and to give His life as a ransom for many" (Mk. 10:45).

The prototype of the woman who serves is the highest of all creatures, who at the moment when she was called to be the Mother of God and thus to the most exalted royal dominion had only one reaction: "Behold the servant, the handmaid, the slave of the Lord." She received the Lord of all life into her womb and bore Him, gave birth to Him, nourished and cared for Him completely in this attitude of self-effacing service. And beneath the Cross she accepted the mission of becoming the Mother of all God's children, and until the end of time she will bear the members of the Mystical Body of Christ, care for them, and raise them in loving service. In imitating the Immaculata there is "for a truly loving wife no longer a problem with taking her place as a subordinate. She lays the firm foundation for a healthy family by her God-fearing, self-effacing, love-enhancing service, which becomes for her husband an example for his attitude toward God and for her children the seedbed for reverence and obedience."[13]

Suffering is profoundly connected with the attitude of service. Ever since the Fall, suffering has been imposed on mankind as a punishment; since the coming of Christ, suffering has become the expression of the highest love:

> Suffering is more deeply woven into woman's nature than into man's. Her nature cannot develop at all except in league with suffering and pain. Indeed, it develops no differently than in mother-

---

[13] Oda Schneider, *Vom Priestertum der Frau* (Abensberg, 1992), 67.

hood. If the woman is privileged to bear children, she must do so through pain. If she is denied children, she bears her fate as a hidden wound within her, which causes her to suffer secretly until her maternal character is released in the opportunity to sympathize with the suffering of other mothers. Virginity, which denies itself physical maternity for reasons related to God, is certainly not an escape from suffering, because it is not a retreat from motherhood. On the contrary: a truly virginal woman has just chosen for herself the spiritual suffering of motherhood, only the care and exhaustion of serving others, while renouncing the happiness of being a physical mother herself: the love of a husband, the warmth of a home, the tender cradling of the fruit of her own womb. For a woman there is no legal detour around suffering, only a path by which to sneak past it, but that leads via the stunting of her nature to the ruin of the good that has been entrusted to her: the family. Where instead of the strength of suffering, a fear of suffering gains the upper hand, where girls or women find satisfaction or see their goal in living as painlessly and pleasurably as possible within the narrow limits of their own ego, then by its very nature full womanhood no longer exists. Being a mother means suffering. A genuine mother does not rebel against it. Indeed, on the basis of her motherhood she is the first to affirm suffering and to be able to overcome it. Because of her natural closeness to suffering she becomes the instructress, within the family and in humanity, for the sublime art of overcoming suffering.

Suffering is overcome on the basis of love. Love leads to suffering, but it also leads out of suffering, because it is stronger than suffering. A mother knows this when she endures the burdens of pregnancy and the pangs of childbirth. She looks beyond them and hopes for the new life, for the great warmth and happiness that it will bring. Her knowledge and hope lead her—the first to glimpse this—to the insight that any and all passing suffering, provided that it is endured correctly, is comparable to those birth pangs, beyond which new life and happiness will bloom. Thus a mother recognizes that suffering is the price of blessedness.[14]

In serving, in magnanimously bearing and enduring the suffering that is imposed, love is perfected. Here love is no longer merely the

---

[14] *Ibid.*, 68.

affective, sentimental, admiring desire to be united with the beloved, but now is effective; it has become a deed, the living gift of oneself. In this way Christ redeemed the world by His coming as the servant of mankind and by His most bitter suffering on the Cross.

By loving and bearing suffering for the beloved, a woman gives life and is in the most exalted sense bride and mother. Just as Christ by His suffering conquered death, sin, and the devil and gave the world the light of the Resurrection and eternal life, so too a woman in union with Mary under the Cross can participate in this radiant new birth to eternal life. By persevering in service and bearing suffering to the end, she causes a ray of eternity to shine in this dark, desperate world. She herself can endure only if she hopes and trusts that her loving devotion will be victorious, that her service will overcome egotism, and her suffering will vanquish the world's craving for pleasure. She can endure the toil of her everyday routine with its thousand annoyances only if she sees them as so many invitations to live out and prove her love. She can do this, however, only by setting her sights on eternity, on heaven as the glorious destination of her pilgrimage through this valley of tears. She can also communicate this often to those who are dear to her. Through her patience and smiling service she brings sunlight to the darkness and warmth to the cold world; a woman is the sign of hope and confidence; her devotion is a perpetual *Te Deum* that concludes with the promising words: "Lord, Thou art my hope; I shall never be put to shame."

Serving Life in the Exceptional Case

Because the ideal planned by God is never completely realized in the world and the consequences of sin often disrupt the order of things, God allows exceptional things to happen in exceptional times, so as to make especially clear His divine freedom to intervene personally, whenever and wherever and however He wants. He then chooses instruments that are unsuitable, especially when viewed in human terms. Just when man goes badly astray, God uses a weak woman "that He may confound the strong" (I Cor. 1:27). But even then He does not abrogate the law that He has established. In considering such examples, like that of St. Catherine of Siena or St. Bridget of Sweden, Sigrid Undset comments: "No woman has ever been a priest; a woman has never received diaconal ordination; a woman cannot minister at the Holy Sacrifice of the Mass, but by the power of the Holy Spirit she can reprimand a priest who dishonors the dignity of his office, even if he should be the Vicar of Christ."

One such example in Sacred Scripture is Judith, who in order to protect the chosen people exchanged her solitude as a widow for the sword so as to perform the bloody heroic deed, since the men of Israel refused. Similarly the heroic deeds of St. Joan of Arc showed how God chose a girl over all the men of her time for tasks that far exceeded her natural gifts and duties and even conflicted with them.

Thus in every age, but especially in times of crisis, there have been such "exceptional services" by women, which of course only go to prove the rule. But in performing duties that were actually typically masculine, those very women gave expression once more, through the contrast, to what is essentially and profoundly feminine. The Maid of Orleans wonderfully manifests the nature of the pure, intact virgin. The extraordinary, actually quite masculine activity of these women is not, as it would be for a man, action of herself and for herself, but rather devotion and self-donation, an extraordinary form of her "fiat." For this reason the women called to such extraordinary tasks always perceive their mission as a heavy cross, and as soon as they have fulfilled the mission or there is no longer any need to replace the man, they immediately retreat again into discreet silence. A woman's home is, after all, the hidden working of the leaven.

The more the world and the Church are in crisis, the more women have to "step into the breach" when there is a lack of masculine strength and men fail to perform their duties. Thus Pius XI speaks in his Encyclical *Casti Connubii* about the necessity of substituting in marriage: "When the husband does not fulfill his obligation, it is the wife's duty to take his place as head of the family." Today, however, we have reached such a chaotic state of affairs that this substitution has almost become the rule.

In this situation, however, it is important that the woman recognize, first, that her "extraordinary" task is an exception and that she should experience it accordingly, while still yearning for her authentic femininity: it pains her to have to do a man's work. If she no longer appreciates this, then she loses her most precious values and becomes a miserable caricature. Second, it is important that she learn to do the man's work, not as the man would do it, but rather as *virgo-sponsa-mater*. What does this mean?

All work by a man is always incidentally a display of his achievement, which is viewed externally as a mustard seed that marvelously grows into a towering tree. As long as he is aware that he is still working only as an image of God, as His instrument, he can be happy and contented with his work. Unfortunately, though, he labors all too often under the ridiculous illusion that the work should be attributed exclusively to him, and even more often he falls into the trap of pride and puts himself, his talent, his own greatness in the spotlight. Here too we find the beginning of his failure.

Therefore if a woman is substituting for him, then that same manly pride must be humbled and his illusion dispelled by the fact that the woman puts herself completely, with her deepest nature, into this work: her power of love, her devotion, her service to life, her "being-leaven." Then she gives herself over entirely to the work, extinguishes her personality, so to speak, so as to be the "handmaid of the Lord" to the last. She thereby counters the man's pride in showcasing his own greatness. Moreover she is still aware also that she must perform here a work that surpasses her natural aptitudes and is constantly overburdening her. She understands intuitively that higher powers must work in her if she is to succeed. She is quite conscious that she is only an instrument, a co-worker; the primary agent and the real author of her work is God Himself. And thereby she counters the man's illusion that he had done the work himself, that he was actually the author.

Precisely the most extraordinary missions of woman in history are the best proof of her knowledge that she herself is completely unsuited to the task and of her complete trust in God; these missions proclaim that He is truly the Mighty One.

Whether in the exceptional cases or as a rule, whenever a woman appears in her threefold nature and lives according to the feminine mission, she testifies to the ultimate meaning and goal of human work: that all work on earth is only service, a collaboration with God's grace; that man is only an instrument and servant of the one who really works, the Lord, and that man is on earth not to glorify himself but rather to accomplish his work for the honor of God and the salvation of souls.

The Sinful Woman and Her Deliverance by Christ

The ideal was crossed out by sin. Sin leads man away from God, causes him to wander from the only path that leads to the goal. Because of sin man goes astray in the talents that he possesses, which he perverts, thus demeaning himself and reducing his work to a caricature.

The same thing happens with the woman who goes astray. Only the error of her ways is quite different from the man's. For her it is mistaken love, for the man it is a mistaken mind and spirit. The man is sickened by vainglory and pride, and his cure must come about through the humbling of his pride; that is why Christ can be so hard on him.

The woman grasps for the forbidden fruit out of mistaken love, in order to be "like God" for the beloved man and to make her beloved husband "like God." The woman's love is directed toward the specific person, behind whom the invisible God has vanished, as far as she is concerned. She has given herself totally to someone who was not capable of accepting her total love, to the man who was supposed to be her mediator with God and not her goal. In her mistaken love it is as if she worships the creature. She is glad that he takes and enjoys the forbidden fruit. From this she concludes that pleasure is the essence and purpose of everything precious in this world, its fruits and its love. Therefore she allows herself to love for the sake of pleasure, and she herself also loves for pleasure's sake.

When a woman forgets in this way her essential tie to God, who endows her heart with the fullness of life; when she loses herself in the world of the senses and feelings and takes this to the extreme in her relationship with the man, then she betrays, so to speak, her most authentic powers and her natural mission. She then seeks to intrude into the man's world and his methods, tries to imitate his organizational and leadership skills (calling it equal rights for women), and labors under the selfsame errors and runs the same risks as the man. By clinging to what is masculine, she stops being man's other half and fails to bestow on him the riches of her soul. Consequently the relation between man and woman becomes unfruitful and the world declines into the typical errors of masculine pride. Today's world boasts of being a world of inventions, economic marvels, and perfect technologies. In civilized countries everything is thoroughly organized in the best possible way. But upon closer inspection it becomes evident that this world lacks kindness, motherliness, mercy, reverence, and tenderness, which of course only a woman can provide.

We have already mentioned the exceptional case, which in our chaotic times has almost become the rule. Therefore it is only right that women today should be teachers, doctors, lawyers, and university professors. Yet there is something profoundly tragic about this: There is an increasing shortage of women in the typically female professions. "No scientist, no artist can fulfill his mission unless the hands of an unselfish woman guard his everyday routine. No physician, however brilliant, can heal his patient if the faithful nurse is missing; no social life can flourish, no home can be a place of security in the absence of the quiet care and service of a woman's hands. Only a woman can manage to resist the depersonalizing trend and loosen up the cold, organizational schemes that debilitate our life today."[15] Consider now the typical woman of today, who to a great extent has lost or betrayed her feminine identity. As a rule she has long since cast off all the symbols of her profound nature: a young woman doesn't understand that language any more. Public opinion is dominated by the fleeting movie star, the beauty queen, or some other sensational female phenomenon. All tactful distance is gone. The reporter does not need to remove a veil; the woman who craves the limelight has already removed it herself. Fashion is all about the undressed woman exposing herself. The purpose of modern cosmetics is no longer to

---

[15] Le Fort, *The Eternal Woman*, 91.

add a certain charm to a bride or to a physically less attractive woman; instead it is designed to erase everything unique about her appearance, erasing her unique charm by plastering it over with a false and empty ideal. Excessively heavy make-up produces an unreal mask that conceals the truth and depth of her personality and makes it invisible and unrecognizable.

The lack of true devotion and willingness to make sacrifices for each other make a man and a woman incapable of forming a strong and lasting bond. That is why the women's magazines are full of stories about unhappy marriages that end in divorce. So the world, with its brutality, its lack of love and fidelity and true values, is headed for ruin. We know that the end times will stand under the banner of the whore of Babylon, whom we have just described. No one should imagine that this is an extraordinary female phenomenon. On the contrary, it is every-day, insignificant femininity that transgresses the divine order: the woman who has ceased to be the one responsible for her eternal symbolic worth, who squanders her vital fullness and precious power to love in countless vanities and conveniences.

What can save her from ruin? Only a renewed consciousness of her primordial powers and essential mission. If she becomes once again *virgo-sponsa-mater*, for the world and for the man, then the sources of life will be opened and there will be new generations of men who respect the mystery of woman and can understand again that in their complementary relation man and woman are the image and likeness of God.

But how can that happen? Man's natural powers are not capable of overcoming the devastation that sin has brought about in his soul and his life. Conversion is always a work of divine grace, which comes to us only from Christ, through the channel that He Himself chose, namely His own Mother.

Thus the Redeemer, the Second Adam, confronts a woman as a specific person, just as the first Adam did. He is capable of awakening her from her sterile addiction to pleasure and to fan again into flame her power to love, to draw her to His Divine Heart and thus to purify her of everything that is useless or evil. He frees her completely from servitude to pleasure. He causes her to be once again what she is authentically according to God's design: devotion and sacrifice. He dies the most horrendous death and by His love to the very end awakens the response of her total love. The woman falls down before Him in the dust and says, "O wondrous Love, O Heart on fire with love for me!" Her love has found infinite room to expand; she has been healed of her thousand erring ways.

Provided that she has good will, Christ will lead each individual woman step by step back to her vital mystery, to her sacred depths. How does Christ accomplish this work of redeeming woman? How does He elicit her love? Just as He Himself said: He does not quench the smoldering wick nor break the bruised reed. In this context that means that He awakens the womanly instincts that are still sound, or at least still somewhat functional, by purifying and elevating them. Thus He leads a woman, however lost she may be, gradually from these remnants of her basic femininity to increasingly more noble responses and behaviors until she arrives at conversion or even sanctity.

How significant it is that for His own coming into the world He chooses a woman who is blessed above all her sisters until the end of the ages. She becomes now the prototype and model of redeemed humanity as a whole; she is, after all, the first to be redeemed. But in particular she becomes the model for women.

He decides to be the child of a mother, to be nourished and protected by her. He knows, indeed, that a woman, however far she may have gone astray through sin, still retains her deepest nature as mother and has preserved the maternal instinct mentioned earlier. In looking at Jesus as a Child, a woman cannot help looking at His mother too, who gives her life for Him, sacrifices herself for Him. And so Jesus runs to His Mother's arms when Herod threatens His life. His childhood is spent in reverence for the womanhood that is manifested in such great modesty and simplicity in Nazareth: the happiness of a mother's love that is forgetful of self, lavish and devoted to service. Meditating on this exalted ideal of the relationship between mother and child profoundly moves a woman in particular and awakens in her the longing to imitate this loving devotion. She is no longer lost;

she has taken the first step out of the prison of her own pleasure. Having glimpsed this maternal, life-giving love, the woman can no longer ignore her desire for it.

In His public life Jesus continues this work of saving woman's soul. This is especially evident in His various encounters with women. Each one is different, although each is connected with a physical or spiritual miracle. For it takes a superhuman power, God's omnipotence, to bring a human being back from his erring ways. And that is precisely why the Son of man came to earth. As with all miracles in the life of Christ, it is true here also that He did not perform these mighty deeds only for the person described in the Gospel; no, through these specific interventions He wishes to demonstrate plainly and clearly that He desires to work in every person of good will. Thus a woman can and should place herself in the situation of a given biblical scene, and even identify to a certain extent with the persons who appear in it, profoundly aware that "You said that to me, my Jesus. You did that for me, my Redeemer."

The meeting with the Samaritan woman (Jn. 4:1-42) shows, first of all, that the Lord does not hesitate to direct his full attention and care to a very ordinary woman and to reveal to her the deepest mysteries of God, despite her lack of comprehension and dignity. We have here before us the type of sinful woman who is ordinary, everyday—indeed, common: focused on the specifics, personally willing to help, interested, grasping the truth intuitively, talkative, unselfish and loving, but also utterly lost in her sins. Christ now latches on to this positive remnant and asks her specifically for an act of charity: "Give me to drink." That is the first move that Christ makes toward the woman. He knows how to adapt to the woman's nature and condescend to the specific circumstances of her life. Here at the well He finds the typical womanly service of fetching water, but also the specific life story of this woman with six husbands. So He looks into the depths of her soul and awakens in her a growing desire for salvation. Now our Lord's second move begins: After He has descended into the depths of her misery and guilt, He gradually lifts her up out of her earthly, sinful life, unlocks her soul, heals her, bestows grace upon her, and transforms her to the point that she can become the apostle to an entire town.

Let us examine this redemptive act of Christ in detail. Given the rather unusual situation that a Jew would have anything at all to do with a Samaritan, much less a woman, He begins by speaking to her with simple words, and then leads her to very lofty spiritual heights: "If you knew the gift of God, and who it is that is saying to you, 'Give me to drink,' you would have asked Him and He would have given you living water." With her intellect the woman can probably understand something of this mighty new doctrine: the main outlines, but not much. Yet these solemn, serious words that are spoken so calmly resonate beyond her intellect in all the depths of her soul and awaken the great longing that she inherited together with her share of Israel's blood: the longing for the Messiah, the longing for the "living water" of redemption. Christ responds to this longing by leading her very subtly to confess her sins, revealing to her the reason for her misery, as if He wanted to say to her: "In giving yourself over to men you were trying to love, but you lost yourself by seeking pleasure in them." He says this without harshness, however, without wagging a finger at her. Her response to this is an acknowledgment of His greatness. Through the immediate impression made by the person of Jesus on her soul, she now experiences decisively such a great thirst for the "living water" that Jesus is able to raise the stakes to the utmost and reveal Himself in a way that He has not yet revealed Himself to anyone, not even to His disciples: "I who speak to you am he."

We cannot tell precisely what happened in the woman's heart at that moment; we can only infer it from the consequences: She leaves her pitcher behind, hurries into the town and announces Him to the people. This testifies to a complete transformation of her soul, and thus to His personal love for her, which has lifted up her errant love and redirected it to its true object, to the Father who is worshipped "in spirit and in truth." Her love, now streaming to its true goal, instantly bears fruit. The woman cannot keep her happiness and joy to herself; she hurries to tell the people and becomes Christ's first woman missionary.

The first healing that Christ performs for a woman is of Peter's mother-in-law, who lay sick with a fever (Mk. 1:29-31). Fever is the best symbol for errant love, the ardor of which becomes trapped in the heart. Love for the wrong object becomes a seething passion, a craving for pleasure that consumes a person's strength fruitlessly and causes the heart to languish for true fulfillment. Jesus approaches the sick woman, bends over her and takes her by the hand. This divine-human hand, full of power and goodness, draws the trapped ardor to Himself, clears a way for it and makes it free and calm. The fever leaves her, and her weakness becomes strength. She stands up and serves. Service to Jesus is the silent language of healed love.

A hemorrhage, a womanly ailment, is the symbol of vital forces that have been squandered uselessly apart from the healthy rhythm of nature. The woman who suffers from it touches the hem of Jesus' garment in faith and thus draws the divine contrary force into her body, which is becoming increasingly debilitated by its weakness. By touching HIM it regains the strength to keep its lifeblood.

The example of the sinner Mary Magdalen (Lk. 7:36-50) is especially moving. The Gospel shows here in particular the whole-hearted, total, and extravagant character of her passions. When such women devote themselves, they give themselves entirely: first in sin, but then in repentance and love. The expression of this total love is her WEEPING. Tears are holy, since Jesus Himself wept.

> Tears are the salty tide of the sea of bitterness that swirls around the shore of mankind which has been separated from God. Woman, having the greater guilt and the more severe punishment, is exposed more to the beating waves of that tide; they constantly play upon her soul, which is easily moved. No wonder her eyes often well up! These streams of tears are a grace which God grants to relieve her. How could Jesus prevent that relief, when a sinful woman was weeping at His feet in loving remorse?[16]

Certainly, as a result of original sin, everything in this life can be misused: "A woman whose errant love has retreated into itself, to her

---

[16] Schneider, *Vom Priestertum der Frau*, 82.

own detriment, egotistically misuses everything sacred, even tears. That is why we must fight against habitual tears, those cheap, petty, egotistical and willful tears, and guard especially against those dangerous feigned tears which in all ages have been the seductive stage-prop of the witch, the instrument of Satan."[17]

Finally, this incident with the sinful woman testifies that when a woman loves, she wants to be extravagant, to pour out the magic of abundance over daylight sobriety: not just to anoint the feet of the Beloved to keep them from getting chafed and sore, but to anoint them so that the whole house is fragrant; not only to take from the jar of ointment what is necessary, but to break it over the feet of the Beloved One and to empty it to the last drop: that is the sign of total devotion. And when the apostles murmur about this extravagance (Mk. 14:3-9), Jesus defends her act with the kindest possible words and promises her the gratitude of the whole world for this disparaged deed of love.

Jesus also healed women of diabolical possession; we get some idea of how serious some of the cases were from the hints about Mary Magdalen, from whom seven demons had to be driven out (Lk. 8:2). It is certain that an abandoned woman is exposed also to this danger in the extreme. Therefore Jesus likes to keep her under His protection later as well. After healing the raving madman, He dismisses him, despite the latter's request to be allowed to stay with Jesus. He does not forbid the women He has healed to become His followers (Lk. 8:2). He knows how much their redeemed love longs to be able to serve Him in person. He knows what this personal connection with Him means to the healed women, that He has become wholly and entirely the source of their strength to resist the evil one in the future. They can no longer live without living for Him.

One day the Pharisees brought an adulteress to Him in order to put Him to the test (Jn. 7:53-8:11). Those malicious men only played into the hands of God's mercy when they brought the miserable, fallen creature to Him, "placing her in the midst." His first glance at her

---

[17] *Ibid.*, 83.

already restored her dignity; His gentle, prudent manner calmed her wild fear; His confident superiority inspired trust, and His exonerating and yet profoundly obliging word of warning quickly won over her sickly love until it rested, healed, in His love. The Evangelist tells us nothing about the behavior of the accused; yet all of her misery and her entire transformation are reflected in what Jesus does and says: hopeless desperation, timid listening, revival, remorse, conversion, and total submission to the Lord.

Besides this great power to love, God has given woman many other gifts that enable her to live out her mystery; we have already mentioned them several times. Just as love goes astray through sin, so too even the most beautiful gifts cast dark shadows of their own. Healing consists, not of throwing the baby out with the bath water, but rather returning from excess or defect to the golden mean:

A woman has to look at everything that is little with motherly eyes, but this can make her petty or fussy. Her orientation to personal matters can interfere with her objectivity and make her curious, gossipy, and conniving. Her task of teaching a child to speak makes her talkative. She cannot be the silent type like the child's father, but must have the words right at the tip of her tongue; otherwise how would the child ever learn to speak? And how would the children ever correct their mistakes if the mother didn't admonish them ceaselessly? But that easily turns her into a fault-finder. Her fine sensibility easily becomes over-sensitivity; her sense of beauty, love of finery and vanity; her sense of honor, effrontery; her spiritual wealth, sentimentality. Her agile temperament deteriorates into moodiness and her sense of modesty into prudery and falsehood.

How, then, is she to find her way back to the golden mean? By imitating the unique individual who attained the ideal. "Look at me and do exactly as I do," said the Immaculata to St. Bernadette as the latter asked her about the way to perfection. This imitation of the Immaculata in the everyday, humble, routine life of a woman contains the key to overcoming all errors, excesses, and defects.

In summary, all that is really necessary is this twofold loving gesture: that a woman should seek to draw near to Christ, that she establish a very concrete, personal, intimate relationship with Him, that she should go to Him in her sufferings and necessities and allow herself to be cleansed often in His Blood which is poured out in love; and that she should go to the Immaculata, who by her example and her all-powerful intercession will most certainly assist in the woman's return from error to truth, in the measure in which she trusts her.

Problems of Women Today

Preserving Beauty

To the materialistic, godless mentality of today's world, virginity is a horror. If the momentary experience of egotistical, sensual satisfaction is commended as the greatest happiness in life, then any human being who deliberately renounces this "happiness" because he believes in another, higher good, becomes a scandal and is treated as an outsider.

Thus a girl who remains true to the great ideal of femininity necessarily experiences the cross of being different. Because she does not go along with the current fashion, with the lifestyle and behavior of "everybody else," she is marginalized, excluded from the group, ridiculed, and humiliated. Because she clings to an ideal and defends it, her behavior is inspected with a magnifying glass, and every failing is severely judged. Often people do not hesitate to provoke her, to parade their own moral filth before her eyes. Now and then some individuals will try in a friendly and seemingly sympathetic way to lure her into the snare, so that she will betray her ideal at least once.

Now it is a common experience that this heated resistance to the individual who goes against the general trend and does not accept "everybody's" opinion is as short-lived as a fire fueled with straw: The straw burns very bright and produces an enormous flame, which immediately subsides as soon as the straw is burnt up. So it is in this case: So many girls give up their ideal because they dread this brutal confrontation with the world, or at least they do not dare to acknowledge their ideal. For fear of public humiliation they just go along. Going along is the beginning of the end: They will not have the strength to resist the pressure from others, and so they are drawn more and more into the worldly mentality, until finally they give up their ideal.

In contrast, the girl who withstands this pressure and does not allow herself to be intimidated by humiliations will very quickly discover that the opposition of the others soon subsides. She is labeled abnormal, crazy, "weird," but they soon tire of attacking her constantly.

Another danger lurks here: a twofold danger. The girl might proudly look down on the others and inwardly judge them as stupid, dirty, the scum of the earth. She could shut herself off from them "since they marginalized me in the first place," and she could take every opportunity to let them know that she is better, more intelligent, and basically more attractive than common folk. Such girls have made their otherness the cornerstone of their arrogance and are well on the way to becoming proud Amazons who don't do themselves or the others any good.

There is another danger for the rather timid girl: She will be inclined to feel like a martyr, a target for the malice of others. So she will shut herself off from others, build her own interior world and thus live apart from reality. This behavior is often combined with silent judgments and commentaries on how bad everyone else is and how there is no point in having anything to do with them. This gives rise to an attitude of antipathy or even contempt. Such girls are in great danger of becoming bitter and spending their lives revolving around their own ego, which is never satisfied and always unhappy.

If a girl is aware of these two dangers and is leading a truly Christian life, she will eventually adopt the right attitude: With regard to the ideal itself she will stand fast and be unwilling to make even the slightest compromise. She would rather let herself be ridiculed and despised than deviate from her principles even an iota. With respect to others, though, she will not for a moment consider herself as "better," since she knows very well that everything she has is grace, love that has been freely given and of which she is not worthy.

The above-mentioned experience of massive pressure from "everybody" and the great difficulties of withstanding it cause the girl to realize that within her circle of acquaintances (for instance in her class at school) there are certainly some who have not resisted this pressure and nevertheless are not yet completely imbued with the false ideals of today's world. Those very individuals, even if there are only a few of them, will be edified by her example, will secretly marvel at her courage, and perhaps would be glad to contact her discreetly.

Knowing that such persons exist, the girl must keep her eyes open and make an effort always and everywhere to give good example. She will guard against commenting immediately on everything and instead will often remain silent, and when she must speak she will pray first for light and strength. She also knows about the important apostolate of smiling, which is not an artificial mask, but rather an expression of good will toward one's neighbor and of the desire to do good for his soul.

Furthermore she will not dismiss everything immediately as bad, but rather will recognize the good beginnings that she sees in the words and actions of others. In personal conversation she will latch on to these "good sides" so as to encourage the individual with whom she is speaking to pursue even more what is good. She will not react to what is obviously bad in others by losing her composure or getting angry, but rather will arouse sympathy, mercy, and compassion in her heart.

Just as the Mother of God had to live in Egypt in the midst of blasphemers and immorality and never said a word, although she suffered unspeakably from it, so too a young woman in the midst of today's sinful world will, like Mary, repay evil with good and overcome the egotism and vices of others through greater love and virtue. Once she has reached this level, the young woman, through fidelity to her virginal ideal, can develop a wonderful apostolate, which we will discuss shortly.

Finding Her Vocation

First of all one thing must be made clear: in order to live a happy, Christian life, it is absolutely necessary to lead it according to the will of God. Every moment belongs to Him; our whole life belongs to Him. And so our state in life, that is, the path that defines our whole life, must also be chosen so as to correspond to God's will. Generally a woman is free to decide between two paths that lead to eternity (for a discussion of the exceptional, so-called "third way," see the next chapter): the usual path of marriage and the special vocation to the religious state. There are indications of a religious vocation when a young woman feels in some special way drawn by God, either to belong entirely to Him, or else to devote herself to His service for the salvation of souls.

Often the actual choice of one's state in life is preceded by a more or less extended period of reflection, discernment, and consultation with experienced, responsible persons. It often happens that an individual tries to make such a choice but still does not get a clear answer. During this interval a good rule is to remain open to the will of God and not to embark on a path because of external influences, acquaintances, advice, or emotions which, for all one knows, may not be in keeping with God's will. Many vocations are ruined by such hasty and reckless steps, and thereby the person himself blocks off the way to a truly happy life. Waiting on the will of God is very difficult, given the pressures of today's world, in which even a growing child is overwhelmed with emotions and feelings that make an objective decision nearly impossible.

Once the choice has been made, a new phase of life begins in preparation for the new state of life. If the vocation is to devote oneself entirely to God, then a very personal relationship with Christ must be developed, an abiding in His Presence. One helpful way to do this is faithful meditation on His personal love for His elect, beloved bride. This love is the precious pearl for which one leaves everything and is ready to sell everything. It is the profound mystery in the heart of Christ's bride, which she carefully preserves and entrusts to no one who has not been called. During this time of preparation, however, she must remain open to her neighbors; she is still in the world, although she is no longer of the world. That is why she will have to distance herself from certain social circles, places, and activities, if these could endanger the precious treasure of her undivided love for Christ. She flees from the noisy world and seeks seclusion and discretion.

If her vocation is to marriage, then the young woman absolutely must realize that God knows from all eternity the bridegroom appointed for her. With unconditional trust in Him she will pray that she might find him. Moreover she should realize that the path of earthly married life is only a temporal one, and that therefore the ultimate goal, beyond all earthly love, is God's eternal love. Love for the earthly Thou can never be an end in itself, but only a path that leads to the supreme, eternal love, to the divine THOU.

The Major Problem of Finding the Beloved Thou

Why is it so difficult today to find a specific partner for marriage? First of all because many people are afraid of making a decision that would bind them for their whole life. The instability of the current age, the complete lack of steadfastness and perseverance, and the almost countless examples of ruined marriages inspire fear. All the more so because young people today, both men and women, are weakened by the poison of the contemporary mind-set: There is hardly anyone nowadays who has not been affected by the pornographic trash that surrounds us and by all sorts of other sins resulting from the satisfaction of the senses and instincts. Psychology tells us that a lack of discipline in enjoying food, as well as alcohol, drugs, rock music, computer games, immoderate use of the television or Internet, etc., weaken the character and the natural strength of a human being and make him incapable of the sacrificial life that marriage and family require.

A young woman, especially one who is trying to maintain her ideal of femininity and wants to become a good wife and mother, is pained by the feminization of men. The above-mentioned traits of today's mind-set make him incapable of being a firm support and providing protection. In searching for a person who still does to some extent correspond to her wishes, she must before all else give priority to a great trust in God. "You know everything, and the more faithful I am to You, the more surely You will grant my prayer." Next, she should not constantly have this important question uppermost in mind, but should tell herself again and again: "I have my duties; I have the will of God to fulfill here and now." Above all she should remember often that everything passes and that only one thing really counts, namely becoming holy. This knowledge about the "one thing necessary" enables a human being, first, to live in the truth and to grasp anew every day the meaning of his life and to actualize it. Next one needs to maintain an attitude of openness: A young woman must not close herself off and simply wait passively for a miracle. God works, but He usually works through secondary causes and most often through quite ordinary everyday events. That is why she should gladly accept all honorable invitations, when she knows that the event will be attended by decent people. Perhaps it is God's will that it should happen there.

But how should she search? A fundamental rule of morality applies here: One must not try to achieve good by using a means which in itself is bad. The noble good of a worthy Thou, a companion for a lifetime, will never be found in an atmosphere of sin. Such places should be avoided at all costs. In contrast, events such as youth group meetings, days of recollection, family celebrations, invitations from good friends—for example, birthdays or other similar celebrations—are certainly good soil in which honorable friendships can grow. In Poland the fact is very well known that for years many young people have found one another during the pilgrimage on foot to Czestochowa. They have a beautiful tradition there that married couples who had their wedding last year wear their wedding apparel and take their place at the head of the solemn procession leading the pilgrimage group, as a sign of thanksgiving that the Mother of God arranged for them to meet each other.

The Specific Choice of a Husband

The biggest mistakes are made, however, once an acquaintance has been struck up. Intimacies begin all too quickly before the two really know each other. Flirting nowadays is almost a normal accompaniment to many meetings of young people; they allow themselves without inhibition to be led by the feelings of the moment, which as a rule make a person blind to the true nature of another. These emotions are the mortal enemy of an earnest familiarity and smother any possible deeper relationship before it can develop.

The young woman often thinks that she can win the good will and attention of the young man only by displaying her charms and allowing him to fulfill his sensual desires with her. The opposite is the case: On the one hand the man shows by such behavior that he is incapable, at least for the moment, of genuine, deep friendship, because he is too deeply entangled in sensual egotism. On the other hand, however, the young woman loses his respect (and that of other men), because she surrenders herself as an object of pleasure. If she responded instead with noble restraint to such "solicitations," then she would not only contribute to the prevention of many sins, but also attract the attention of nobler men, which likewise could be an important element in finding a suitable husband.

After the initial acquaintance comes the phase of learning more about one another and getting closer intellectually through conversations and written contact. They may proceed to the first expressions of affection only after both have said an initial, provisional yes to the possibility of life together, to the question of whether they are made for each other. As long as this first, provisional choice has not taken place, the young woman is free to date several men. Once the choice is made, however, she must concentrate on the one who will become her Thou.

Now a time of intensive examination must follow: principles by which to live, character, temperament, ideas about the details of family life, attitude toward religion and morality, interests, connections with others, reading and hobbies, family and circle of acquaintances—all these things must be analyzed thoroughly; this is an intellectual task that requires a clear, cool head.

Now what are the criteria that should guide this discernment? First they should realize that there is nothing perfect on this earth. What is important, therefore, in observing the other's qualities is not the success that he or she has attained, but rather a constant and consistent effort to do good and avoid evil. The other party is good if he or she honestly and steadfastly endeavors to be good, if his or her spiritual and moral foundation is firm, even if there is still occasional failure to apply those principles in practice. A reliable touchstone is one's answer to the question: "What do I expect from the other? Am I myself willing to give it?"

How many relationships that began well are shipwrecked because the young woman discovers a weakness in the young man and is now "disappointed with him." Here she must ask whether this disappointment is even justified. If she looks a little deeper, she often sees that her thoughts and feelings were actually guided by her own pride. She dreamed up for herself an ideal of a perfect prince and is now "disappointed that he is no different from the others." Precisely here it is so important to make a distinction: Was he weak because he has no firm principles, because he really didn't make any effort at all and his "convictions" were only superficial, for show? Or was he weak because even the best man is weak, but he is heartily sorry for it and is working with all his might to improve and in no way means to deny his genuine convictions? In the second case she must forgive him magnanimously and regard it as her task to help him to overcome the weakness. Only in the first case should she break off her relationship with him as quickly as possible.

Often a woman's choice is determined also by externals and superficial criteria: physical strength and macho behavior, friendliness, a feeling of security and closeness, a handsome, manly appearance, etc. All that means little if there is no underlying spiritual foundation, which can be summarized in a few central concepts: fidelity, submission to the will of God, especially in what concerns the man's natural duties as husband and father. And to probe even deeper: In a human being there are two basic and opposite attitudes that determine everything that he thinks, says, and does in life: egotistical concern for self first, and self-donation to a beloved Thou. Very soon it becomes clear which of these basic attitudes prevails. Only when the clear and constant decision for self-giving, for true love, has been made fully and completely can one begin to trust such a person.

Disappointments

It is part of human nature that every new discovery is a pleasant, beautiful experience that brings joy. This is true especially when one "discovers" a good person and receives his affection and interest. It is also only human to present one's best side to such new acquaintances. When two people then have already decided on one another and are preparing for marriage, then they will make even more of an effort to give their best, if only out of fear of disappointing or even losing the beloved.

Once the honeymoon is over and the newlyweds have grown accustomed to each other, the charm of "novelty" automatically fades and gives way to everyday life. This transition is always a painful experience. Furthermore, this same daily togetherness very quickly uncovers hitherto hidden faults and bad habits in the other. We know from personal experience that thoroughgoing changes in life can cause problems and character faults to disappear as though overnight, because one applies oneself intensively to something new that is completely captivating. This is especially true when people fall in love: What was previously so important and engrossing suddenly becomes unimportant and is forgotten. Once one has become accustomed to the new situation, however, the intensity diminishes also, and one is no longer completely absorbed, and behold, the old errors and weaknesses that were supposed to be gone suddenly reappear on the surface. They were not dead but only asleep. This is precisely what happens in marriage after the first months. What's worse, it disappoints the expectations of the spouse. How often one must listen to the rebuke: "If I had known that, I would have thought twice!"

Very often another important, well-known factor adds to the difficulty: Every man has a special relationship to his mother, especially if she was a good, caring mother. As a married man he must reconsider and find a new relationship to his mother that is in keeping with his devotion and duties to his wife. For many men this is a very heavy cross, which unfortunately is usually not made any lighter by the mother or the wife. The will of the one to dominate and the jealousy of the other almost inevitably bring conflicts into the married life that has just begun, and if the couple is not careful, this can prepare the way for catastrophes in the future.

It is extremely important to resolve these initial conflicts and marital problems immediately. To many people they seem "not worth mentioning" and so this baggage is heedlessly carried around; the spouses do not notice that they are undermining the foundation that they have built together. These difficulties that are not resolved at the outset are often the real reasons for failed marriages and ruined families.

Basically one must always keep in mind the deepest nature of marriage and family. The idyllic situation implied by mindless films and romance novels is a deceptive picture that no one should even dream about. The Christian understands from the outset that life, whatever form it takes, is a way of the Cross, and this way of the Cross and each of its stations must be accepted in advance. Many women have become saints through the difficult sufferings and sacrifices resulting precisely from their marriage. Perhaps the best known example is St. Rita.

A wife who knows this will not have exaggerated expectations of her husband, but will always be conscious that the law of love is to give without counting the cost.

Practically speaking, when the honeymoon is over, both spouses will try to live their usual routine in light of the Holy Family. Love grows through sacrifice, through the many thousand efforts to serve the other, to bear with his weaknesses, to do what pleases him. Only these thousand little sacrifices can assure that the two never become bored with each other, but rather deepen their married life, love, and care for one another more and more and support each other on the long way to the heights.

If an unknown, previously hidden character flaw should come to light, both will be able to distinguish between it and the genuine depths of the person, who indeed desires what is good and sincerely wants to be a perfect spouse and grieves that he has still not achieved it. St. Paul's maxim applies here: "Bear one another's burdens." If, for example, there has been an outburst of anger or a bitter exchange of words, then the spouses will not hold it against each other, but rather will understand that that is not really the nature of the other, but only remnants of the "sinful Adam" who just has not yet completely died and rears his ugly head every now and then. "Do not let the sun go down on your anger." As soon as the storm is over they should sit down together and calmly discuss what happened, forgive one another and resolve to do better the next time. If they do that, then the frequent little marital squabbles will be no obstacle, but rather an occasion for better understanding, mutual assistance, and love.

If the "wife vs. mother-in-law" problem should arise, the wife must fight in particular against the temptation to jealousy. Here, too, frank discussion is very important, for often the husband does not really notice what is going on in his wife's heart and then wonders why she acts irritably and thus unconsciously vents her anger or jealousy. Moreover this problem appears in reverse when her own child comes into a woman's life and the young mother has to concentrate on her little one and so neglects somewhat her devotion to her husband. Now it is his turn not to give in to jealousy and the feeling of being neglected, but instead to endure this new situation in the spirit of sacrifice and devotion to them both.

Therefore, if one looks carefully at these marital problems, they are all without exception excellent opportunities to fulfill the word of the Lord: "If anyone loves Me, let him deny himself, take up his cross each day and follow Me."

The Greatest Disappointment

The moral chaos of our time and the disruption of the moral order affect in particular the willpower of young people and their ability to make decisions. They have become almost incapable of making a firm commitment because everything changes so quickly and they themselves no longer have any stability. For this reason their fear of a marital commitment is understandable. This is especially oppressive for a woman, whose fertile years are limited. The experience of broken marriages, the infidelity of spouses, and disappointing relationships with men gives her an almost instinctive reluctance to keep searching. Thus on the one hand she is resigned, while on the other hand she is deeply pained by her lack of fulfillment. The great joy of finding someone after all is often muted by the deep wounds of the many "lost" years or the impossibility of having many children.

Her disappointment is complete, however, if she does not find a husband. For this reason many women go through obvious or hidden depressions. She may try to outmaneuver the pain by keeping herself occupied in various ways—in frenetic activism, in an artistic, refined lifestyle, or by using various "substances" in order to forget. In a similar situation, some women convert but are faced with a hopeless family situation (divorced, separated, misunderstood, and intellectually spurned by her husband, etc.). Like a sword, the self-accusation pierces her heart: I have wasted my life; everything about me is sterile, fruitless, meaningless. Is there any help for such women, who are quite numerous today, or are they doomed to vegetate in their misery?

Experience shows here that superficial attempts at a solution produce no results; on the contrary, they usually drive the person deeper into spiritual misery. The only ultimately valid solution is found in the Lord's words: "There are those who refrain from marriage for the sake of the kingdom of heaven. He who is able to receive this, let him receive it" (cf. Mt. 19:12). Only Christ solves the problem, redeems the lonely woman's life, and reveals to her a completely new plan of life. A review of the basic principles of human existence enables the woman to reflect in depth on her situation: "Why am I on earth? If the prime of my life is already past and I have still not been able to find a beloved Thou, then isn't God trying to tell me something? Isn't that a hidden invitation that brings my whole existence to a previously unimagined new level?" Indeed, "God is faithful," and "one day for Him is like a thousand years." "He desires that all men be saved" and attain their perfection. And so He issues His call to the soul. Unceasingly and at every moment the light of grace falls upon the hearts of those who open themselves to Him. There are laborers who went into the vineyard at the first hour, but others too who went at the sixth, ninth or even the final hour. But all of them receive the same wage. Behind the futile search for fulfillment in the world, year after year, suddenly HE appears, touches the soul and says to her, "You are mine!" It is never too late to devote oneself completely to Him. All the natural womanly powers that cry out for love, yearn for security, and desire to be fruitful and have children, are not ruled out but are redirected to a greater love and fruitfulness. Christ Himself personally becomes her THOU. This love for Christ is an espousal with all the characteristics of spousal love: undivided, permanent, and fruitful. What the lonely woman thought she could not find is granted to her: security in Him. Looking back on her life, most women have to say: "No man could have cared for me better than He; no family life could have made me happier or fulfilled than my task with Him and for Him."

Nevertheless a hidden lament remains: Why couldn't I have experienced this calling earlier? Why did I have to live for so many years in uncertainty about my vocation? And isn't this choice of Christ somehow a substitute for the husband that I didn't find? The answer to this is the principle that God's ways are not our ways; His thoughts are not our thoughts. He calls however and whenever and wherever He wills. But then there is another answer derived from the situation in our world today. The more the world sinks into the chaos of godlessness and increasingly large sectors of human life are deprived of the structure of family life or religious community, the more God grants special vocations to carry His light even to places where the previously normal paths no longer lead. These are vocations of persons who do not leave the world yet live in it according to the evangelical counsels, the so-called "third way," which has been approved explicitly by the Holy See.[18]

---

[18] Pius XII, Apostolic Constitution *Provida Mater Ecclesia* (1947).

The Third Way

The Christian world order was constructed upon two pillars which form the basis of the natural and spiritual family: marriage and the religious state. These apocalyptic times are characterized by an unprecedented spiritual confusion that casts people out into the world alone as victims of their longing for happiness, which is now promised them as a paradise on earth. Thus a human being loses his way in the vicious circle of restless this-worldliness, which is divided into working for the moment and enjoyment for the moment. He becomes a spiritual orphan who needs protection and devoted love more than other children. He has turned away from the family; he has no contact with and no confidence in priests and religious. Who will look for these lost sheep, which are so numerous?

This is where the "third way" comes in: the consecrated life of laity in the world, which once was quite rare but is increasingly common today. Without habit or veil a human being lives as a bride of Christ, a living tabernacle in a desert where faith has grown cold, a lonely worshipper amid profanities and obscenities. Where no priest can make headway today, a woman consecrated to God can establish the kingdom of God. "God alone knows what good has been accomplished by such girls and women and what evil has been prevented by the mere fact that they, with their virginal commitment and courageous consent to their lonely way, purify the overheated atmosphere from lewdness."[19]

Indeed, what is there today that can still touch a person who is alienated from God and the truth? Often the only thing remaining is good example, the quiet consistency that does not allow itself to be stopped or discouraged by any obstacle or ingratitude. That is why God calls magnanimous women to be "light in the darkness" in caring for the sick and the elderly, in the fields of education and social work, and generally anywhere a motherly heart can resist contemporary egotism, set an example of the ideal of devotion, and be a dis-

---

[19] O. Mosshammer, *Priester und Frau* (Freiburg, 1958), 191.

penser of life in the deadly atmosphere of a world that is growing colder and colder.

This vocation is genuinely feminine: unassuming, hidden, discreet, requiring perseverance and a motherly sense of mercy. Precisely because a woman with such a vocation receives no outside protection but is stationed in the midst of a dangerous world, she needs all the more a profound spousal relationship to Christ. She has to be a bride of Christ in the deepest sense, the spiritual mother of souls, willing to be consumed for HIM unto the end. This is the third way, but in a sense the first, because it demands the most love.

Apostolic Work—Spiritual Motherhood

Whether it is along the third way just described as a vocation, or during the virginal phase of life in which she has not yet decided upon any particular state of life, a woman is always called to apostolic service, that is, to spiritual motherhood. She is beset by the question: "How in these dark times can girls and women be led to the light of their nature?" A woman desires to give life. For her all people are in some way children to whom she wants to give the true, everlasting life. Her glance falls first on other women who unconsciously still retain something of the depth of their authentic nature, as evidenced by their longing for beauty, for fulfillment in love, for motherhood. Even in perversion it often comes through like a ray of light in the midst of the darkness: sometimes compassion with the weak and unfortunate, on other occasions care for others, good advice, etc.

To bring these unconscious desires to light, to help a woman be glad that she is a woman: that would be the task of the spiritual mother. To use the beginnings that are available so as to awaken in a woman the beauty of her maternal, spousal, and virginal qualities. In doing so today, she must always start with generally accepted insights or her own personal experiences, so that her conversation partner can follow her train of thought and corroborate it with her own experience. The description of great female personages can be very helpful in this. Sometimes a "personal connection" can help here also, for instance, the patron saint of the conversation partner.

There is another very special application of woman's spiritual motherhood: her care for the priesthood. Lu is a poor village in Northern Italy. In 1870, eight mothers from that locality pledged to receive the sacraments once a month and to pray for an hour in the afternoon at a private house. Their intention was to pray for good, holy priests and religious for the Church. They kept their pledge for eleven years. As of 1881 the village had its own pastor, which gave new impetus to the mothers' cause. Soon there was not a single woman left in Lu who did not participate in the monthly "Vocation Sunday." The result was at first an extraordinary increase in the number of Catholics who received Holy Communion. Then—and this made Lu famous—there was an astonishing growth of vocations. The parish in Lu has given the Church no less than 500 priests and religious vocations.[20]

This little example—one among many—shows how much women feel that they share responsibility for the priesthood. The priest is the mediator between God and men, the conveyor of divine life, without which no one can be saved. There is no higher form of spiritual motherhood than to awaken a vocation to be a priest. God hears the prayers of His own, and He wants there to be not only physical but also spiritual mothers of priests, who through their prayers and sacrifices give birth, as it were, to the priesthood in the soul of the man called.

All these various kinds of spiritual motherhood, in other words, of the apostolate of women, receive a very profound impetus from the work of the "Militia Immaculatae" of St. Maximilian Kolbe. The ideal of the "Knight of the Immaculata," as he describes it, gives a woman a wonderfully simple, handy structure in which she can carry out her apostolate. In view of the superior power of the evil foe and his earthly accomplices, we must clearly understand, on the one hand, that we are much too weak and pitiful to resist his attacks by our own strength and to keep the faith; and, on the other hand, that God has given the Immaculata the power to crush Satan's head and

---

[20] *Ibid.*, 321, 113.

to vanquish all the heresies throughout the world. This is what God is calling each of us to: as members of the Church Militant to enter into the fray and to help spread the true faith, to work for the building up of Christ's kingdom and thus to save souls. He has granted all these great graces to the Mediatrix, the Immaculata, who is His preferred instrument, the channel through which all graces of conversion and sanctification flow to the souls that need them.

Now the Immaculata too, ordinarily wants to distribute these graces in a certain way, and so she rallies her faithful children and knights around her; dependent on her and totally consecrated to her, they become instruments in her immaculate hands. Thus she exercises her spiritual motherhood in a marvelous way: She is the real mother of souls, who in them gives birth to divine life, sanctifying grace. She does this, however, through her instruments, her knights, who thus also play an essential part in the birth and preservation of eternal life in souls: in Mary her knight is called also to spiritual motherhood. Now this is true in a very special way for a woman, who indeed in her inmost being is already an image of the Immaculata. Her spiritual motherhood is the noblest sort of fruitfulness and the fulfillment of the feminine mission, as all the holy women testify who have performed such great services for the salvation of souls, down to St. Theresa of the Child Jesus, who became the patroness of the missions because she was so thoroughly a mother of souls, because she was completely an instrument in the hands of the Immaculata.

Practically speaking, a woman can be an instrument and a knight of the Immaculata at any place, in any situation, at any time. For the individual knight who "endeavors to realize the purpose of the Militia Immaculata individually according to his own circumstances and the rules of prudence,"[21] a woman might be an example to those around her by her fidelity to the ideal of *virgo, sponsa,* and *mater,* but now fully conscious of her complete dependence on and consecration to the Immaculata. Furthermore St. Maximilian recommends that the

---

[21] St. Maximilian Kolbe, letter dated May 25, 1920, quoted in K. Stehlin, *The Immaculata Our Ideal* (Warsaw: Te Deum Press, 2005), 130.

knights cooperate in a common apostolate, because one can achieve more and work more effectively in the world by united effort. Thus girls and women could form a simple organization (student group, youth movement, etc.) for the purpose of enabling women who are inspired by a high ideal to meet and support one another and to remind each other about the essential importance of the Immaculata and of devotion to her. Moreover they could influence other girls and women of good will through the print apostolate (a newsletter) and a wide variety of common causes. How many young women owe their acknowledgment of the truth and of the great ideal of womanhood to the example and apostolate of other girls, without whom they would have never found the way!

Finally, St. Maximilian presents the idea of heroic, total devotion to the Immaculata: the unrestricted consecration of one's whole life to this spiritual motherhood as the property of the Immaculata. He gathered knights who had committed themselves to this total consecration into "Houses of the Immaculata" and the "City of the Immaculata," whereby the knights sealed their total consecration through religious vows.

Is it not possible that there are women who in their longing for a life of virginity and spousal union with Christ might discover God's call to devote themselves unreservedly to becoming "mothers of souls" by consecrating themselves unreservedly to the Immaculata? With that we have arrived again at the "third way" described above, with the important addition that a woman can be a hundred times more certain of success in apostolic work and lifelong devotion through the great insight of St. Maximilian Kolbe, namely, "being an instrument in the hands of the Immaculata."

Conclusion

Your life is only a short exercise in mountain climbing. It is God's will that during this short time you yourself reach the goal, namely the fullness of your womanhood, that you do whatever is in your power so that others too might recognize this, the only true destination, and that you stand by them so that they do not tire along the way and are not overpowered by dangers. But since we are all weak, helpless sinners, we have the lifelong task of liberating ourselves from errors and of striving always with God's help to reach higher ground by fulfilling our duties better.

Your task is to let the ideals of virginity, spousal union, and motherhood reach fulfillment in you, knowing that these are simply the threefold expression of your love, which should increase constantly until death. But it increases only:

IF you keep alive within you the actualized ideal of womanhood, the Immaculata, and her faithful icons. Therefore meditate often on the example of the holy women of all times and pray that you may follow in their footsteps regardless of what other people around you say or do.

IF you yourself arouse and preserve in your heart the yearning to become an ever more faithful icon of the Immaculata.

IF you direct your unbounded power to love and your womanhood entirely toward Christ and love Him immensely as your "Way, Truth and Life" just as Mary Magdalen loved Him. This is possible, though, only if you constantly get to know Him better, meditate on Him, and thus fall in love with Him in trembling reverence, with all the strength of your heart. Take Him everywhere with you, discuss everything with Him, give Him everything, and trust Him blindly. Keep watch and pray also to avoid and to remove everything that contradicts this love or in any way could diminish it.

IF you entrust yourself entirely to the Immaculata. She should be your prototype in everything, especially in your devotion to God and mankind. Go to her at every moment, find in her your great dignity and a taste for everything that is truly beautiful and pure. Live in her, the Virgin of virgins, the Bride of the Lamb, the Mother of the whole Christ, both the Head and the Mystical Body.

In that way you will bring all creation home to God in your heart through Mary.